How To Have An Instant Massage Therapy Practice

The *REAL* Truth About What It Takes To Get Hired, Attract Clients, And Be Successful In Any Economy That Your School Didn't Teach You

Jeff Sauers

How To Have An Instant Massage Therapy Practice

Copyright © 2013 Jeff Sauers

First published 2013

Printed by CreateSpace

Email: jeff@instantmassagetherapypractice.com

www.instantmassagetherapypractice.com

Printed by Createspace

How To Have An Instant Massage Therapy Practice

Jeff Sauers

ISBN-10: 1494497581
ISBN-13: 9781494497583
Library of Congress Control Number: 2013923394
CreateSpace Independent Publishing Platform
North Charleston, South Carolina

DISCLAIMER:

Although the author and publisher have made every effort to ensure that the information in this book was correct at press time, the author and publisher do not assume and hereby disclaim any liability to any party for any loss, damage, or disruption caused by errors or omissions, whether such errors or omissions result from negligence, or any other cause.

❧ Dedications ❧

To my wife Cheryl. Without her help and support this book
would never have happened.

—

TABLE OF CONTENTS:

———

INTRODUCTION

"This Is NOT What I Was Told It Would Be Like"

Let me tell you a story about my friend Mary...

I came home from work one evening after a really good day. I had a pretty full schedule. My last client ended at 7 and by 7:30 I was in my sweat pants sitting in my lounge chair, feet kicked back, a beer in one hand and a slice of pizza in the other, watching Goodfellas for the zillionth time.

As soon as I settle in, my phone rings. I usually screen my calls but when I saw a particular number appear, I immediately jumped up. It's my good friend Mary. I didn't hear from her in about two years. She's always fun to talk to. She's one of those people you feel that you're best friends with as soon as you meet her.

"Jeff! It's Mary!"

"Mary! How' are you? It's been forever since we've talked" I excitedly said.

"I know" she said. "I've been meaning to call you for a long time."

"So what's going on?" I asked. "What have you been up to?"

"Well, I changed careers recently" she said.

"No kidding" I said. "So what are you doing now?"

"You're never going to believe this, but I'm now a massage therapist just like you!"

I hesitated for a moment before I answered. Mary's also been known to be a kidder.

"Seriously?" I finally said.

"Yep"

"For how long now?"

"I got my massage license about 9 months ago."

"What made you decide on that?" I said finally believing her.

"Well, you know how I've been frustrated with my job lately?" she said.

"Yeah, I kind of remember you saying that the last time we talked." I said.

"I've had it. I was sick of working these incredibly long hours, my boss is a jerk, and my work just wasn't satisfying anymore. And I always noticed how happy you are in your career. You choose your own hours, charge a very respectable rate, it's relatively stress-free, and no one is standing over your shoulder giving you orders."

"Well, yes."

"So I started really thinking about it and called a few schools. They gave me statistics about how much the massage therapy field is expected to grow in the next ten years. And I'm seeing more and more day spas opening in my area. They wouldn't be opening if there wasn't a need for it, right?"

"Um... yes and no. All of that is kinda true" I tried explaining to her. "Except what you don't understand is –"

"So I took a leap of faith and enrolled in massage therapy school."

"Wow!" I said, still not really knowing what to say. "So how did you like school?"

"I loved it!" she said enthusiastically. "It was sooo different from the corporate world. Everyone was nice. My instructors were great. Some of the students even told me that I have a natural feel for it. I mean, I picked things up so easily. I don't know how to describe it, but I think I was really meant to do this for a living. It just feels so right."

"I'm so happy to hear that, Mary" I said. And I was. Mary is a true people person and a real go-getter. When she has her mind made up about something there's no stopping her. And her bubbly personality will definitely help to attract clients.

"So how's everything going so far? Are you working anywhere? Building a clientele?"

"Well... not really. That's what I wanted to talk to you about." Mary said. She now had a worried tone in her voice.

"So what did you do first right after you got your license?" I asked.

"The first thing I did was write a very professional letter of introduction and sent it to every place I could find that offers massage therapy. I even followed up with phone calls asking if they received my letter. No luck. I worked on some family and friends hoping that they would tell others and I'd get some referrals from that. Nothing happened so far."

"Did you try to find your own private clients?" I asked.

"I got business cards printed and I handed them out every chance I got. No one is calling me. And even if someone did call, where would I work on them? The best I can do is set my table up in my living room. I don't have a room in a place like a hair salon to practice from and I can't afford to rent space yet. I thought I'd just keep trudging along. Something will break sooner or later."

"Did you eventually get your foot in the door anywhere?"

"Three months later I finally did. I'm practicing part-time out of a chiropractor's office and a hair salon. I have some regular clients but my schedule is still erratic. Some weeks are pretty busy and other weeks are pretty dead. I'd love to practice massage full-time, but I can't give up my day job. And the clients that I've worked on so far LOVE my sessions, but I'm not getting referrals from them.

Well, I got a couple but I mostly have to rely on the doctor and the hair salon to supply me with clients. And honestly, they're really not doing much of anything to get new patients/clients."

"Are you doing anything more to find clients on your own?" I asked like a lawyer who already knows the answer to a question.

"I still hand out my business cards to family and friends, and even give away some free on-site massage but very little comes of it and I'm finding that it's not worth the effort. Every now and then I mail out my resume to other establishments hoping that someone might be hiring, but nothing ever comes of it. There's also a lot of competition in my area and the economy still isn't that great."

I can hear the optimism quickly leaving her normally chipper voice.

"This isn't how I thought my massage career would be almost a year after graduating. I don't get it, Jeff. I thought this was supposed to be a growing field? I don't know what else to do to get clients. I mean, I'm giving away sessions for free and STILL not getting many appointments from it. I'm starting to wonder if going to massage therapy school was even worth it. This is not what I was told it would be like."

This is not what I was told it would be like. I can't tell you how many times I've heard that from struggling massage therapists.

"Mary, why didn't you call me months ago? You know I would've steered you in the right direction."

"I dunno. I guess I thought that the advice from the schools and from what I read in the trade journals would be enough".

"Um... not really."

"What do you mean?" she said with a concerned tone of voice.

"I'm gonna let you in on a little secret. The massage schools and organizations purposely don't teach the real information you need to know to get a room to practice from how to easily attract clients."

"Huh?" she said.

"Yeah. It's pretty easy to get a practice going with clients already scheduled for you. Anyone can do it easily. They just don't teach anybody how." I said matter-of-factly.

"What?!" she screamed. "Why the hell not?!" she demanded to know.

I took an extra second to put down my beer bottle build a little anticipation before I answered. "... it's because they don't know it."

There was an awkward silence. I could tell Mary was getting more frustrated by the second.

"I don't get it. I'm confused."

"You and the rest of the massage community."

Mary's story is unfortunately far too common. Most therapists go from dreaming about a wonderful new career, to long periods of frustration, and inevitably stop practicing all together.

Without having ever met you yet, I bet you fall into one of these three categories:

If you are a current massage therapy student, you're probably thinking...

> *"What a wonderful career I'm about to enter into! I'll get to help people relax and feel good for a living. And I won't need to work a 40 hour week to make good money. I can be my own boss. And according to my massage school, the massage industry is booming. They even gave me statistics from the U.S. Department of Labor and the AMTA.*
>
> *I can work in a day spa, doctor's office, gym, hair salon, tanning salon, etc. I can even be mobile and go to people's homes or offices if I wanted. I can also rent space and open my own practice. I won't need very much space. This is going to be great!"*

If you are a fairly recent massage graduate (*let's say within the last 6 months or so*), you're probably thinking...

> *"Boy – finding a job as a massage therapist is tougher than I thought it would be. I've been sending out my letter of introduction to every business in my area that offers massage and no one is hiring. I mean, how can I work on people if I don't have a room to practice from?*
>
> *I finally got a couple of part-time shifts at one of those massage franchises. The commission is a lot smaller than what I thought it would be and I'm not very busy, but I guess you have to start somewhere.*

Maybe I'll be able to get more work after I learn more techniques. I can't afford to open my own place and I can't seem to get my foot in the door anywhere else. In the meantime, hopefully this place will pick up and I'll keep my eye out for any other places that might be hiring."

If you are an experienced massage therapist, you may be having thoughts similar to this...

"I've been licensed for the past 5 years. I've also continued my education. I now do Swedish, reflexology, aromatherapy, deep tissue, hot stone, and even on-site massage. I'm practicing part-time out of a chiropractor's office and a hair salon. I have some regular clients but my schedule is still erratic. Some weeks are pretty busy and other weeks are pretty dead.

I'd love to practice massage full-time, but I can't give up my 'normal' day job. I get a few referrals here and there, but I mostly have to rely on the doctor and the hair salon to supply me with clients. And honestly, they're not doing much of anything to get new clients.

I hand out my business cards to family and friends, and even give away some free on-site massage but very little comes of it and I'm finding that it's not worth the effort. Every now and then I mail out my resume to other establishments hoping that someone might be hiring, but nothing ever comes of it. There's also a lot of competition in my area and the economy still isn't that great.

This isn't how I thought my massage career would be at this point when I was in school. But I guess that's just the way it is."

Sound familiar? I know in my career I've had *ALL* of these feelings and experiences. Unfortunately, most therapists can't find any work, can't get enough work, can't get paid what they should, or can't attract enough of their own clients.

It feels like a trap you just can't seem to get out of, doesn't it? Sitting at home waiting for the phone to ring isn't any fun, especially when you love what you do.

The truth is that the vast majority of massage practitioners are underemployed, feeling as if they have to scrape and beg for clients and have to settle for whatever work is offered to them – *if any is offered at all.*

They graduated massage therapy school with the false belief that handing out business cards, flyers, brochures, giving away free massage samples, placing an ad in their local paper and sending out cover letters to day spas and doctors' offices is the path to a fulfilling career.

The reality is that they're left feeling frustrated with little or no clients of their own, no good job options in sight – and no money in their pockets. Many massage practitioners have no choice but to either give up altogether or supplement their income with another job.

I understand. I've been there myself.

I was a practicing massage therapist for 16 years and during that time I've worked for chiropractors, general practitioners, osteopaths, an on-site chair massage business, popular day spas, a massage franchise, as well as eventually having my own mobile and private practice.

I've performed massage in every environment you can think of from doctors' offices to business offices, hair salons to elite day spas, convention centers to outside events, hotels to bed & breakfasts, gyms and girls' night out parties, in studio apartments and $1,000,000 homes, radio stations and malls... *even a bus terminal!*

In the beginning of my career, most of the employment I've received or clients I've generated was from sheer hard work, determination, persistence, and admittedly, getting lucky by being at the right place at the right time. There were even times when I couldn't work on people because I didn't have a room to work out of.

So just like you, I know the frustration of not knowing how to find a room to practice from, how to attract clients, and feeling forced to rely on others for my income who didn't have a *clue* how to attract massage clients.

It still amazes me that no one has ever turned the process of getting a room and attracting clients from scratch hasn't been developed. Until now.

I've been in this field for 20 years and as of this writing, <u>it all boils down to 4 things that massage therapists want</u>:

1. They want a room to practice in without being forced to rent commercial space.
2. They just want to do massage and not learn copywriting or marketing.
3. They want client-attracting techniques that are on a showstring budget or free.
4. They want clients to come to them.

So I've decided to write the most practical, real-life, quick and easy guide ever written that shows massage therapists how to attract client *immediately* without feeling awkward and uncomfortable about the process.

I walk you through the process of how to get a room to practice from, how to get new clients by having others promote you, and how to keep a massage practice going no matter what the economy is.

But I must caution you: this isn't a comprehensive home-study course. There are many aspects of having a successful massage practice that I *DON'T* cover such as referral systems, social media, advertising, the business side, etc. I only go into the hardcore basics that you NEED to know right now that will get your career off the ground.

But if you only implement these techniques alone, you're gonna have a highly successful practice fast!

So if you're thinking about choosing massage therapy as a career or are currently in massage school or even if you are already practicing massage, this book is for you! It is a practical, real-life, no airy-fairy book that will open your eyes to what it *REALLY* takes to secure a room to practice from and how to attract clients quickly and easily.

So grab yourself a drinky-poo and get comfortable. Your about to discover the easiest and fastest way there is to attracting clients that isn't taught anywhere else.

And relax. It's not your fault you don't have enough clients.

Chapter 1

HOW TO EASILY GET A ROOM TO

PRACTICE IN

***"If Massage Therapy Is Supposed To Be Such
A Growing Field, Why Are So Many Therapists
Unemployed Or Underemployed?"***

That's a real good question. It doesn't make any sense. I mean, massage therapy is supposed to be rapidly growing, right? I'm sure your massage school gave you statistics from the AMTA and the US Department of Labor showing how much our field is expanding.

But there *is* one missing piece of the puzzle that no one tells you...

No one tells you how to separate yourself from your competition to actually <u>land a room to</u> practice in to *get* your career off the ground!

All of the client-attracting information I've purchased already assumed that *ALL* therapists already have a room to work out of.

In all my years in our industry, I've found that one of the biggest hurdles we all have to overcome at first is finding a room to practice in to begin with. I mean, there's no way to help people if we don't have a room to practice in, right? This is especially true if you're a current massage therapy student or a recent graduate.

You see, most massage therapists don't have a clue about getting their "foot in the door" for a job opening... not a clue. Forget about job offers... most therapists see months fly by without landing ONE decent job interview!

This is a big shock for recent massage graduates. They go out into the world with this false belief that all they have to do is send out a generic letter of introduction and they'll get sufficient employment. Then reality sets in...

They either get no phone calls, or at best, maybe a room to practice in but little or no clients. Then they get very disillusioned about the massage industry. They start to wonder...

> **"Where are all the massage jobs? I thought this was supposed to be such a growing field?"**

So if you've faced this problem yourself, again, I want to reassure you that...

It's Not Your Fault!

You simply weren't taught how to get yourself established somewhere and how to easily attract clients!

And not only that but...

If you ask experienced massage therapists if they're happy with the amount of clients they have and/or what they're getting paid, I can assure you that the vast majority of them will say, "no" even from therapists who have been in practice years!

Again – why is this so? And even if you get lucky and find a job as a therapist, why is it so hard attracting clients if our field is supposedly expending? Well, I want to reveal something no one else has yet...

As of this writing, I've been in the massage industry for 20 years and believe me, I've purchased my share of client-attracting books, courses, seminars, etc.

However, I realized that there is a massive void and also a *huge* opportunity for therapists that no one is noticing...

It Seems That Businesses Who Offer Massage Don't Have *Any* Clue How To Effectively Market Massage To Their Existing Clients!

For example, salon owners don't know how to market massage to their clients. Chiropractors don't know how to market to their patients. Gym owners don't know how to market to their members.

For many years, I worked in these same frustrating environments. I *knew* that there was a great opportunity for all of us, if only *anyone* knew how to market better. I know *I* didn't know how to do it at the time. I promoted myself the same way every other therapist did with little results.

But What's Worse Is That I've Talked To Many Doctors And Managers Of Gyms And Salons Who *Used* To Offer Massage, But Stopped Only Because They Just Couldn't Figure Out How To *Market* Massage

So *believe* me when I tell you that business owners are *craving* for someone to come in and show them how to attract massage clients. I've had *dozens* of them tell me this during my career.

But the problem goes even deeper than that. Many therapists don't even have a room to work out of.

Most of them can't afford to rent space, so the only other alternative is to contact places that offer massage just to get themselves set up somewhere.

And the usual ways that therapists look for a room is to cold call businesses or send their resume and letter of introduction.

This rarely works. And what usually ends up happening is that they either give up completely, or settle for any work that's offered – if any is offered at all. Then they end up in this trap they can't seem to get out of.

And this is a problem that I've found in other marketing courses – they assume that everyone already has a room to work out of. But in my experience, too many therapists have a difficult time just getting their foot in the door anywhere.

So now I want to reveal...

Why Almost *All* Letters Of Introduction And Resumes From Even The Most Experienced Therapists Get Thrown Out And How To Avoid It

This is the little-known job search secret that is guaranteed to get your phone ringing with interviews even if you're just out of massage school. Nothing happens — and I mean NOTHING HAPPENS — until your phone rings for the job interview. Landing that first job interview is priority #1! This is where ALL of your focus needs to be. *(Read that again)*

How is this done? Easy. The secret is...

A Powerful, Carefully Written Cover Letter That Speaks
The Language Of The Business Owner Will Fill Your
Calendar With Quality Job Interviews Faster And Easier
Than You'd Ever Imagine... And Even Get You A Higher
Commission Than A Therapist With 10+ Years Experience!

Why? Because your cover letter is the ONLY chance you have to make yourself stand out from your competition for the opportunity to even be interviewed for the job.

A Brilliantly Worded Cover Letter Is, Without Question,
The Fastest, Easiest, And Most Sure-Fire Way To Get A
Business Owner's Attention And Get Your Phone Ringing...
And Practically No One Understands This Fact!

Not only that, but most cover letters do nothing to land the job interview.

One of the biggest problems that chiropractors and salon managers face is the barrage of letters of introduction and resumes they constantly receive.

But the *biggest* reason why almost all these letters and resumes get thrown out is because they...

Offer Absolutely Nothing New To The Business!

Why should they call *you* over any other resume they receive?

You *MUST* stop and think to yourself...

"What's In It For Them?"* or more accurately *"Can You Generate Clients?"

This is the *ONLY* thing that managers *really* want to know – can you bring clients? *That's It!*

What many therapists don't realize is that...

The Number Of Hours Your Training Was, The Number Of Techniques You Know, What Organizations You Belong To, Or Your Past Employment History *Doesn't Matter!*

Now, the typical letter of introduction (*or cover letter*) usually has the practitioner's name, title, address and phone number at the very top. It then goes on to say things like how professional they are, the techniques they know, how often they're available, and how well they work with others.

If they're experienced, a resume is also included. And they *all* say the same thing, which is basically *"give me work"*! I've got news for you – it isn't how 'professional' your letter is, how many techniques you know or even how experienced you are that's going to get you noticed.

Well, it matters a little, but what managers are *really* looking for is...

"Can You Generate Clients? What Will You Do For Me? What's In It For Me?"

Think about it for a minute. Put yourself in the shoes of the average day spa owner. Let's say you want to add another therapist. You have a choice of 2 therapists to choose from.

You can either pick:

Bob – A very experienced, well qualified therapist, but doesn't know the first thing about marketing and is expecting *you* to fill his shifts.

Or...

Mary – A recent massage graduate who only knows Swedish and has no prior work experience, but has a solid marketing plan that shows *exactly* how she's going to market to your existing clients and also how she's going to attract new clients, sell *way* more gift certificates, start a referral program among many other things – and *none* of this is going to cost you, the owner, a dime.

Honestly which one would you bring on board? Mary is the obvious choice. *Why?* Because Mary has a greater chance of bringing your day spa *much* more business and profit than Bob does.

I Can't Tell You The Amount Of Therapists I've Met Over The Years Who Know A Dozen Different Massage Techniques And Have Been Licensed For Many Years, But Are *Always* Scraping For Clients *Or* Employment

That's Why...

You Can Be The Most Qualified Therapist In The World, But It Doesn't Mean A *Damn* Thing If You Don't Know How To Attract Clients!

It's as if you might as well not know any of those massage techniques. And knowing this little inside information can get you into establishments who claim they aren't looking for therapists at this time, which leads me to the next point.

You see, what an owner or manager *really* means when they say they don't have any openings is:

"We don't have enough clients to keep another therapist busy. There's just enough work for the X number of therapists we already have."

That's the actual truth, whether they consciously realize it or not. But that doesn't mean *all* the massage rooms are busy *all* the time. It's just that they can't generate more clients on their own to keep another therapist busy.

Big difference! You see, even the "busy" day spas don't have *all* of their massage rooms filled every hour. So it's not like there isn't space for you, it's that they don't believe that they can keep another therapist busy. Maybe they're having a hard time keeping their current therapist(s) busy.

After many years of observing this, I started thinking of the typical ways that therapists look for a room – either cold calling businesses or mailing the same old "professional" letter of introduction and/or resume and getting little results. You know the one...

"Hi. My name is Mary Smith and I've been a licensed massage therapist for the last 5 years. I'm a member in good standing with the AMTA. I attended the USA School of Massage with 1,000 hours training. I also continued my education by studying aromatherapy, reiki, sports massage, and reflexology. I feel I have a lot to offer your business. I have an outgoing personality and work well with others. My hours are flexible. If you have any availability for a massage therapist, please contact me at..."

Basically, *"give me work"*. Of course, now you know why this goes directly into the *"special file"*. So I thought if I found a way to write a letter of introduction that explains what I'm going to offer their business, chances are high that I'll get interviews. Makes sense, right?

I also knew that this wasn't enough. You can't make empty promises just to get your foot in the door. A solid marketing plan *must* be ready to go. If I then showed them a plan that shows them how *I'm* going to generate massage clients, I'd probably have my pick of businesses to choose from!

So how *do* you get the attention of a business that offers massage and convince them to give you a shot? This is easier than you think *if* you know the secrets to speaking the language of the owner or manager, which I'm going to reveal in a minute.

One day I came up with a way to craft a letter that if *I* were an owner of a business that offered massage, I'd almost *have* to at least call this person for an interview. When I was finished writing this *radically* different letter of introduction, I thought I really cracked the code as to how to get a business owner's attention.

However, I wanted to get the opinion from others to really validate this. So I showed this letter to a few chiropractors and day spa owners I knew and asked them what they thought. I didn't tell them what I was up to, though. I just asked them to read it and let me know their opinion of it.

The answer I got from everyone without exception was...

"Wow! Who Is This Person?"

I then asked them if they would call this person if they got a letter like this in the mail. They ALL enthusiastically said *"absolutely"*! In fact, every one of them said that they *wished* they received letters like this from massage therapists.

Let's move on now to the perfect letter of introduction...

Chapter 2

8 STEPS TO THE PERFECT LETTER OF INTRODUCTION

And now the moment you've been waiting for! Here is the formula for the...

1. **<u>Strong Headline.</u>** The most important part of your letter is the very top. You DO NOT want to put your name and contact information as the very first thing they read. Why? Because in all honesty, *who cares!*

   You *must* start with a powerful, benefit driven eye-grabbing headline that immediately captures that person's attention and practically forces them to keep reading.

   Let's say you wanted to mail a letter of introduction to a hair salon that offers massage. <u>An example of this type of headline could be:</u>

   "Would You Like A Massage Therapist On Your Team Who Consistently Generates Clients For

**Your Salon Who's Not Just Sitting Around
Waiting For You To Give Them Work?"**

Now if you were an owner of a day spa and received a letter that had *this* headline at the top as opposed to the typical name and contact information that *every* other resume has, wouldn't you continue reading?

Wouldn't you want to know who this person is?

But having only your name and contact information at the top simply doesn't pique their interest enough to keep them reading.

2. **Empathy.** The next thing you need to do is tap into that business owner's frustrations. The way to really keep their attention and get them hooked into you is by identifying what problems they're having with their massage therapists.

    An example of this could be:

    *Are you sick and tired of massage therapists who aren't willing or don't know how to stimulate a steady flow of clients for your business, yet expect to be highly compensated?
    Are you frustrated with one identical resume after another from therapists which basically say, "Give me work"?*

    I guarantee that this will practically force them to continue reading. How could it not? This is a problem that every day spa and doctor who hires massage therapists has.

3. **Your Introduction.** *Now* is the time to introduce yourself. Too many therapists make the mistake of talking about

themselves *first* before getting the attention and identifying with the problems that that business owner has.

However, now is *not* the time to start rattling off your grocery list of massage techniques that you know. Save those details for your actual resume. Keep it simple and describe your education in a very conversational tone.

Remember - what they *really, really* want to know is –

"What can you do for me and my business?"

Which leads me to the fourth step:

4. **Stating Exactly What You Want.** This is where you're really gonna set yourself apart from every other massage therapist looking for a room. And guess what? *You're NOT looking for a job!*

   You simply tell them that you're looking for a room to grow your massage practice in. You're not looking to *"get hired"*.

   You're looking for an establishment where you can grow your massage practice that will be mutually beneficial for both them and you. Tthis takes a huge burden off their shoulders.

   Think of it – you're not *at all* asking them to supply you with clients.

   You're going to do all the marketing, which leads me to the fifth step:

5. **What You Will Do For Them.** Next, describe in short bullet points some of the things that you will do for them.

   A few examples are: Starting a marketing plan that will easily turn their existing clients into massage clients, implementing a client referral program, and showing them how local businesses will promote them like crazy, among others.

6. **Describe What You Won't Do.** For example, you won't expect them to provide your income, you won't sit around being unproductive during down times, or make up excuses if you don't produce the results you promised. Who else makes a statement like that? *Absolutely no one!*

7. **Give Testimonials.** Next, include about 2-3 testimonials from people you've worked on. They don't have to be long, you just want to impress the person reading this. You can say something like...

   "And here are what just a few of my satisfied clients are saying about my massage sessions..."

   And *no one* includes testimonials in their letter of introduction or resume. Wouldn't that impress you if you were a day spa owner?

8. **Set A Time Frame.** If you want to really impress them like no one else has, set a time frame to accomplish this in.

   You can say something like...

"If you are not 100% satisfied by my progress within 60 days of working with you, feel free to terminate our arrangement with absolutely no hard feelings whatsoever."

Now, imagine if *you* were a day spa owner and read *this* kind of letter of introduction. You'd almost *have* to call this person and want to speak with him/her, wouldn't you? This would be the *perfect* person you'd want for your business.

This therapist isn't going to be sitting around waiting for you to fill their schedule, they're coming to the table with their own marketing strategies, and they even gave themselves a time frame to accomplish it in!

How could *anyone* not want to bring this person on board?

And this is very difficult for massage therapists to accept because they think, *"I don't know how to get clients. I just want to do massage. I'll let someone else do all of that stuff"*.

How To Find The Right Room For
Your New Massage Practice

First, make a list of every establishment that offers massage therapy in your area, such as day spas, chiropractors, hair salons, gyms and tanning salons.

*(NOTE: Do *not* write down the names of any well established fancy-schmancy day spas. I'll explain why later on. Look for smaller, independently owned ones)*

This is easily done by going through your phone book and also searching online. After you have a list of places that offer massage therapy, drive by a few of them when you can.

If you have the time, walk inside one of them to see what a certain establishment looks like. Is it clean? Does the staff seem friendly?

<u>And here's a very important question to ask yourself</u>:

"Would I get a massage at this place?"

Imagine if *you* were someone thinking of getting a massage somewhere. Would you pick this location? And if not, why not? Try to get a general feel of the place.

Seeing the inside of every establishment isn't always easy to do, especially with doctor's offices. But do the best you can. Day spas and hair salons are the easiest to view.

The ideal place to find is one that has a comfortable vibe to it. It should be the type of place that you'd like to be associated with. You should be able to come up with a general list of places quickly, even if you haven't seen the inside of most of them.

Let's assume that most of the places that you contact will be day spas and chiropractic offices. Which one should you choose? <u>There are pros and cons to each</u>...

Hair Salons/Day Spas

<u>**Pros:**</u> You're almost guaranteed a tip. Everybody knows to tip when they get a haircut, manicure, pedicure, facial, waxing, or massage. It's rare if you don't get tipped. Also, you can package

your massage services with the other services that the salon offers.

This skill alone will position you *way* ahead of your competition. This type of environment is also perfect if you enjoy doing relaxation types of massages like Swedish, Hot Stone and Reflexology.

Cons: Depending on the income level of your community and the economy, it might be tough for some people to spend money on things like massage, facials, manicures, etc.

It's also harder to promote what I call 'fix it' type massage therapies like Craniosacral, Myofascial Release, and Neuromuscular Therapy. People naturally associate day spas with relaxation and pampering as opposed to getting 'fixed'.

(*On a side note, the line between a day spa and a hair salon that offers many services often blurs. There is no real distinction between the two. Once a hair salon starts to offer services like massages and manicures, they automatically call themselves a 'day spa'. Some do, some don't. In many cases, a hair salon and a day spa are one in the same.*)

Chiropractic Offices

Pros: Able to accept health insurance. Many health insurance companies will pay, at least in part, for therapeutic massage. This is an incredible benefit for you because you're more able to see clients on a consistent basis without them running out of money.

It's very common to work on clients once a week or sometimes even more. You're also able to do the 'fix it' type of massages.

More people will see you for headaches, chronic neck and shoulder problems, lower back issues, herniated discs, etc.

So if you enjoy working on these types of problems, a chiropractic office would suit you better.

Cons: Forget about getting tips. You get them occasionally, but people don't associate tipping with a doctor's office – especially when their health insurance is paying for their appointment.

It's also harder to promote the typical hour-long relaxation type of massage at a doctor's office. The environment of most doctors' offices is pretty sterile and boring. They usually don't have the same comfortable feel that a day spa does.

You'll get more business promoting half-hour long massages that focus on issues such as neck and back problems as opposed to an hour-long relaxation session.

Now that you know the pros and cons of each, this information will put you in the driver's seat.

If you don't feel comfortable with an establishment for any reason, you won't have to take whatever is offered just because it's available.

Here's Another Tip For Finding A Room...

If you're having difficulty finding establishments that offer massage therapy, you can always run an ad in the classifieds that says that you're a massage therapist looking for a room in a chiropractor's office or hair salon to use for your massage business.

However...

Do NOT say that you're looking for work!

State in your ad that you'll be generating your own clientele. This is *very* important. You're *not* looking for work! Remember that.

Other establishments that you could check out are:

- Gyms
- Tanning salons
- Rehabilitation centers
- Doctors *(other than chiropractors)*

Not all of them offer massage therapy, but some do.

The *ONE* Letter That Gets Day Spa Owners, Doctors, And Gym Owners To Stop What They're Doing, Knock Over Their Coffee Racing To The Phone To Interview You... No Matter How Inexperienced You Are

After you have a list of places that offer massage therapy, you want to now send them a cover letter about yourself.

But this isn't going to be the typical cover letter that you're used to seeing. You already learned earlier in this chapter why that style doesn't work.

On the following page is an example of a cover letter that is guaranteed to get any employer's attention and inspire them to pick up the phone and call you over any other cover letter or resume they've received!

**Would You Like A Massage Therapist On Your
Team Who Consistently Generates Clients For
Your Day Spa And Who's Not Just Sitting Around
Waiting For You To Give Them Work?"**

Dear Mrs. Johnson,

Are you sick and tired of hiring massage therapists who aren't willing or don't know how to stimulate a steady flow of clients for your business, yet expect to be highly compensated?

Are you frustrated with one identical resume after another from massage therapists which basically say, *"Give me work"*?

Wouldn't it be great if a massage therapist came to you with effective marketing strategies that bring in a predictable stream of clients and continuous fresh ideas ready to implement without having to rely on you for their income?

**Finally There's A Massage Therapist That Guarantees
To Increase Massage Clients For Your Business**

My name is Karen Jones, and I've been a licensed massage therapist for the past four years. I'm a member in good standing with the AMTA. I have also continued my education by becoming certified in Neuromuscular Therapy from the St. John's Neuromuscular Institute as well as becoming certified in Shiatsu from the Ohashiatsu Touch For Peace Institute in New York.

I am looking for a day spa where I can grow my own massage practice that will be mutually beneficial for both the day spa and for me. I have numerous cutting-edge, proven marketing methods that are ready to be implemented immediately.

Here's what I will and will NOT do:

I *Will*...

- *Set Up Joint Venture Arrangements With <u>Local Businesses Who Will Eagerly Promote Your Day Spa For Free</u>*
- *Implement A Proven Client Referral/Reward Program To Jump Start Business Immediately*
- *Design Creative Massage Packages That No Other Day Spa Or Massage Therapist In The Area Offers*
- *<u>Increase Gift Certificate Sales By At Least 20%</u> Using An Inexpensive But Highly Effective Method*
- *Drive More Traffic To Your Web Site*
- *Print My Own Marketing Material So There's No Cost To You*

I *Will* Not:

- *Expect You To Provide My Income For Me*
- *Sit Around Being Unproductive During Any Down Times*
- *Use Old, Traditional Marketing Techniques That Don't Work*
- *<u>Make Up Excuses If I Don't Produce The Results I Promised</u>*

I have a positive, friendly, proactive attitude that will make your day spa a more enjoyable environment for you, your staff and your clientele.

If you are not 100% satisfied by my progress within 60 days of working with you, feel free to terminate our arrangement with absolutely no hard feelings whatsoever.

Enclosed is my resume of complete training and work experience. References are also available upon request. If you feel that

I can be a positive addition to your business, I can be reached at (555) 555-5555.

Thank you for taking the time to read this letter, and I hope to hear from you soon.

Sincerely,

Karen Jones, LMT

Read this as if you were an employer and notice how radically different it is vs. the typical *"give me work"* style cover letter. I'll then point out why this works so well.

I lead off with a powerful headline – not my name, initials, address and phone number. That alone will grab their attention and force that person to keep reading.

I then used the *Problem-Agitate-Solve* technique by speaking their language and pointing out how great it would be if they had <u>a massage practitioner who was proactive in creating their own work</u> – not sitting around waiting for clients to fall in their lap.

Now that I have their attention, it is only then that I briefly introduce myself and give a quick summary of my education. I then point out in *exact detail* what I will and will not do for their business.

I make myself look even more desirable by giving them a strong guarantee. If they are not 100% satisfied with my progress within 60 days of working with them, they can let me go without any hard feelings whatsoever.

What other massage practitioner offers their potential employer a 100% guarantee and a timeline to achieve it?

Now if *you* were a day spa owner, <u>wouldn't this letter grab you by the shoulders, shake you and practically force you to stop what you're doing immediately and call this person</u>?

Even if there weren't any openings at this time, wouldn't you at least want to meet the person who wrote this letter and keep him or her at the top of your mind when an opening does arise? You'd be *insane* if you didn't.

If I were an owner of a salon or small day spa, I would actually create an opening for a person who was as proactive as this. And trust me, many will.

If you sent out a letter like this knowing that you have the marketing skills and knowledge to accomplish all the promises you've made, you're practically guaranteed to have your choice of places to practice from.

This is how a massage practitioner who is fresh out of school will get establishments to call them over experienced massage practitioners.

Pointing out *what's in it for them* carries more weight than a grocery list of modalities that almost all massage practitioners have anyway.

Here's another little test you can do to prove this for yourself:

Send out ten cover letters or resumes in the same format that everyone else does and send out ten cover letters in the format I just showed you and track your responses. The difference will be clear.

With this style of cover letter, you can now interview day spas and doctors instead of them interviewing you! You will be in a much better position to negotiate your commission because they will quickly see what you will be bringing to their business.

And believe me, *NO* other therapist that they've heard from is doing anything close to this method. They all give their leverage away by acting as an employee, accepting any work that's thrown their way.

Not You!

You're a professional, and you're going to approach them in a way that they'd be foolish not to make room for you. You will walk into an interview glowing with confidence because you'll know you don't have settle for whatever they may offer you.

You'll actually be looking at their establishment through the eyes of a renter. You'll be able to kick the tires, so to speak – like you do at a car dealership. If you don't like what you see, you don't set up shop there. Simple as that.

At the risk of repeating myself, most day spas aren't as impressed with the amount of education you have (*although it does play a factor*) as much as how much business you can generate for them. It's simple economics.

They'd much rather have a therapist who only knows Swedish massage but knows effective marketing skills that can consistently bring in work as opposed to a therapist who know 7 or 8 modalities but has no clue how to attract clients.

Oh – and here's why shouldn't you send this letter out to the well established day spas in your area: The main reason is because they're simply not going to allow you the marketing freedom you'll need to generate clients. They're just not going to let you do what you wish.

Also, they're not going to alter their pay just for you, even though you have a solid marketing plan that no other therapist has in place. They already have their way of doing things and that's that.

Not only that, but you'll have absolutely no access to their database, even though *you'll* be the one who will be attracting many of their new clients. Like I said in the introduction – *dumb dumb dumb* owners and managers.

So why should you give away your marketing skills to a well known day spa when...

A) You're not going to be paid any more than the other therapists
B) Won't have access to the names and addresses of the clients that *you* attracted with these marketing techniques, and
C) Won't have the freedom to implement this system anyway? Believe me when I tell you that you are nothing but a cog to them, as harsh as that sounds

However, a smaller local hair salon, day spa or chiropractor will, in most cases, allow you to do all of this.

They recognize that:

1. You're the one with a great marketing game plan
2. You're the one who is taking the initiative to put these ideas in motion without relying on them to do it for you *(which they'll love you for)*
3. You're the one doing not only all of the marketing but the hands-on work as well
4. You're the one bringing all or at least some of the supplies you'll need *(table, linens, oil, etc.)*

5. The more work that *you* generate, the more money *they'll* make! Remember, the vast majority of them are *dying* for a massage therapist to present them with these exact ideas that you're going to learn throughout this course

With all due respect to these business owners, 99% of them have *no clue* how to market themselves properly. They just use the same old, worn out traditional marketing methods that every other type of business uses with little or no results.

And as I mentioned earlier, if you were a business owner who offers *(or wants to start offering)* massage therapy, wouldn't *you* be seriously interested in someone who is presenting you with these fresh ideas and won't just sit back waiting for you to supply them with work?

Wouldn't this be the massage therapist of your dreams? There's no doubt that the answer is *yes!*

After you've found work space that you'd enjoy having a massage practice in, what's next?

Chapter 3

TURNING THE TABLES: HOW YOU

INTERVIEW ESTABLISHMENTS

Let's assume that you've found a hair salon that you can use for your practice. The room is nice, the owner is open to your marketing ideas *(which you'll learn shortly)*, and it looks like a good arrangement for everyone. What do you do next?

First, let me tell you what *not* to do. Don't simply put out business cards and brochures on the counter the way every other therapist does. You're just wasting your time and money. You won't get clients that way. You need to be proactive and take matters into your own hands by first introducing yourself to the staff.

What you want to do now is to give a letter of introduction to everyone who works there – the stylists, the receptionists, the nail techs – everyone. Briefly introduce yourself in the letter and offer each person a free half-hour sample of your massage session.

This accomplishes two things:

1. You'll get to personally meet every single employee at the salon. They'll now be much better acquainted with you and know first-hand what your massage sessions are like
2. These people will soon become your ambassadors and will be eager to promote you (*more on how that's done shortly*)

Wouldn't this be the massage therapist of your dreams? There's no doubt that the answer is *yes!*

I want to now go back to the beginning for a moment to help you out in what to say when you first meet with the day spas and chiropractors who want to meet with you to discuss your practicing massage at their location.

If you're the type of person who gets real nervous about going on interviews, this will put you at ease. The truth is that *you're* actually going to be interviewing *them*. Remember, you're not trying to be an employee. You're looking for a room where you can set up your practice.

It's difficult to put an exact script together because every situation is different, but when they start asking you exactly what you have in mind, you can say something like this:

> *"What I'm looking for is a place where I can set up my own massage practice. I already have a marketing plan in place, so you won't have to worry about supplying me with enough clients. However, I would like the opportunity to be able to market myself to your current clients and let them know about my new massage practice here in your salon."*

At this point, you shouldn't be feeling any resistance. No smart business owner would keep you from marketing your practice to their clients. That would only take money out of their pocket. 99% of them would think, *"Hey – if you know a way to get more business out of my clients, I'd love to hear more. I could never get a massage practice going here before. If you think you can, go for it."*

You can now explain how you first want to offer all of the employees an introductory massage session. Then you'd like to provide to every client an introductory massage offer that either the employees hand out or that can be mailed out.

Remind them that you already have this in place and ready to go, so they won't have to do anything except look it over and give you the ok. And it won't cost them a dime. No costly advertising needs to be done.

Tell them about the ways you have to get new massage clients to rebook. Then explain your various referral programs that can be tested. You can then tell them how you plan on reaching cold prospects and winning them over.

You can even have a collection of your promotional material that they can view. This will really knock their socks off! Imagine how impressed you'd be as a salon owner if a massage therapist came to you with all this? How could you not want to work with this person?

When it comes to money, a 60/40 split is best but a 50/50 split is fine. Don't go any lower than that, and don't let any of them talk you into a lower cut. Remember, you're NOT an employee.

Heck, you might not really care for the establishment once you get a good look inside. That's why you should view this process as if you're a renter, not someone who's looking for work. There's a big difference.

Also remember not to jump on the first offer you get, especially if you're not fully convinced that this might be a good place for you. Look at a few places if you can. After you've mailed this cover letter to your mailing list and are starting to go out on interviews, exactly what do you say?

It's difficult for me to suggest what to say at this point in time because you haven't finished reading this course yet. Once you have, you'll have a much better understanding of what to say and how you're going to present yourself.

Every person and every situation is different, but this will help to give you an idea as to what to say once you're there. But you're going to feel *much* more comfortable once you know that you're the one in control.

However, I *will* give you some tips now as to what to watch for when you go out on interviews.

1. **Ask to see the massage room.** Is it a room that you'd be comfortable working in? If you were a massage client, would you feel comfortable getting a massage in this environment? If not, don't set up shop there even if they offer you shifts.

   Approach it as if you were looking for an apartment to rent. You're not going to like every room that you see and you shouldn't jump on the first one that you like. Remember, you're *not* looking for work!

You're looking for an arrangement where you'll be an independent contractor, not an employee.

2. **Will you be able to keep the names and addresses of the massage clients that _you_ generate?** This is critical! You MUST, without question, be able to keep the names and addresses of the clients that _you_ generated from _your_ marketing ideas and hard work.

   If the salon owner has a problem with this, politely point out that _you're_ the one providing the marketing plan, _you're_ the one who is going to be doing the work, _you're_ the one giving the massages, and _you're_ the one who is bringing in most, if not all, of your supplies.

   If they still have a problem with this, simply thank them for their time and end the interview. Again, you're a sub-contractor – _not an employee!_ You simply need a room to work out of for _your own_ massage business.

   It's understandable if they won't allow you information from clients who are already in their database. But you're not asking for that information _(even though you're still going to be marketing to them as you'll soon learn how to do)_, you just want to make it clear that you can collect and keep the information for the new clients that you generated. They can keep a record, too, if they wish. That's OK.

3. **You determine your commission.** The average split is 50/50. Sometimes you can get a 60/40 split in your favor if the salon owner really loves your ideas and is having a difficult time generating massage clients on their own. But DO NOT go any less than 50/50.

I don't care what they say. If you do, you'll be giving up your leverage. Do not let anyone either bully you or try to talk you into an arrangement that's less than 50/50.

4. **They must give you marketing freedom.** If for some reason they don't like the marketing techniques that you're going to use, don't use their facility for your practice. There is nothing taught in this course that is controversial or that is going to offend anyone.

    If they only want you to market your practice using conventional marketing methods, don't use their space. Remember, it's YOUR massage practice, not theirs.

5. **You must be able to market to their clients/customers.** This is another extremely critical aspect. Again, you're not asking for their names and addresses so that you can "steal" them, you just want to be able to offer your massage services to them.

    Practically all salon owners and chiropractors will let you do this. But if any of them won't, then they are, quite frankly, stupid and you shouldn't agree to use their space for your practice.

    If they don't have the common sense to see that it's much easier to sell to existing customers than to strangers, then they are an establishment that you want to stay away from entering into a business agreement with.

    If you *do* get any resistance from them, don't use their room for your practice. You shouldn't have any problem with this, though.

If you come to them with great ideas and the knowledge to effectively market to their existing database, 99 out of 100 will let you do it.

Just first let the business owner see whatever marketing material it is that you're going to be sending to their clients so that they know what you're doing.

You're going to be amazed at how the leverage is going to be in YOUR favor when you go about looking for a room this way.

It'll actually catch them off guard. They're not used to therapists as smart as this. They're used to therapists settling for whatever scraps of work are thrown at them.

Now it's time for me to sidetrack for a moment to teach you a powerful method...

Chapter 4

THE MOST COMFORTABLE WAY TO INFLUENCE PRACTICALLY ANYONE TO GET A MASSAGE FROM YOU

At this point, I need to sidetrack for a moment and reveal a secret psychological weapon that is the easiest way to convert prospects into clients that I've ever come across in all my years of being a massage therapist.

It's a format that's going to be used throughout this course. You're going to see it tailored toward different groups of people.

I never saw this taught in any other marketing material I've studied. I really want to show you just how easy it is to attract clients even if you're the shyest person in the world.

Once I started using this technique, I just *could not* believe how effective it was. I'm *still* amazed by it. It's a new technique I kind of stumbled upon by accident that I call *The Guinea Pig Method*.

This section is going to seem a little backward because I'm going to show you the format *before* I show you an example of it.

This is because this format is going to be used a number of times throughout this course for different groups of people, and I want you to understand it *first* before seeing it. So bear with me for just a little bit, ok?

The idea for this actually came to me simply by listening to my clients (*And BTW – if you own my prior course or received my newsletters in the past you KNOW how much I stress listening very carefully to <u>everything</u> your clients tell you besides the typical 'my shoulders are feeling stiff' kind of stuff*).

Anyway, one day I was working on a client not long ago – sometime in 2008 after my first marketing course was already released – and I happened to mention there was a new massage technique I wanted to learn.

My client immediately said to me, *"Hey Jeff, if you ever need a guinea pig to practice on, you can always call me!"*

That's when the light bulb went off. I realized that many of my clients throughout the years used these exact words – *'guinea pig'* – whenever they volunteered themselves. Not all of them, but a lot of them did.

Why it didn't sink into my thick skull until that moment, I don't know – but I'm sure glad it finally did. After I got home that night, I started structuring the format of new type of sales letter.

Once I had a basic outline down, I just *knew* I hit a home run. I knew it was going to attract clients like crazy. Before I tell you what I wrote, let me give you a few phrases I DID NOT use because they're so cliché and over used and, well, they just don't work.

Things like, *"Massage Therapy Now Available"* and listing every massage modality I knew like *"Swedish – Deep Tissue – Reflexology – Aromatherapy"* and *"50% Off Next Session"* and phrases like that.

I wrote a letter that looked as if I was writing a personal letter to just *one* person – not a letter that was obviously going to a mailing list. This is very important. You don't want your letter to appear as if it's going to a large herd of people.

I started off by using courier font *(that's the font that looks like it came from an actual typewriter. It gives off a more personal feel)*.

I opened with a large and very compelling headline to get their attention. I didn't start the letter with my name or the name of my practice.

I asked them how they were and hoped everything was ok. I then asked if they'd like to be a *guinea pig* and receive a half-hour sample of my new massage session I've created in exchange for their feedback.

I also told them that I wanted to thank them for being such a great client by offering them this complimentary session and I also thought that they would appreciate being one of the first to experience it before anyone else.

Then I described in detail the exact benefits they're going to feel from this session. I don't say, *"Would you like to try my new Myofascial Release session for free"* – which is what most therapists do. Why not just word it that way? Because when you look at it through the eyes of a client or prospect – what the hell is 'Myofascial Release'?

Not only that, it just describes the feature, not the benefit they're going to feel as a *result* of receiving Myofascial Release (*or whatever it is you're offering*). Very important!

I wrap it up by giving a time frame for them to take advantage of this in before I offer it to the general public. I'm going to give you a few examples of this type of letter shortly, but first let me give you a number of psychological reasons why this format works so well.

1. Asking for their feedback in exchange for the massage. What a lot of therapists don't realize is that when you offer a massage for free or for a dramatic discount, people subconsciously think, *"what's the catch?"*

   Many massage therapists don't realize this.

   However, when you give them a reason why you're making this incredible offer – in this case, it's in exchange for their feedback – they're more at ease at taking you up on your offer.

2. People LOVE giving their opinions. Asking others for their opinion is a sure-fire way to get responses. I mean, who *doesn't* like giving their opinion? We all do.

You genuinely want to know what they think of your massage session.

3. <u>Thanking them for being a great client</u>. Another secret to keeping clients feeling bonded to you is by simply thanking them for being such wonderful and valued clients. It's so simple and yet so few businesses do it. In this case, you're rewarding them with a discounted or complimentary massage for being great clients.

    They're not expecting it – meaning that for every 9th massage they get their 10th one free. Not that there's anything wrong with that kind of promotion, though. But recognizing how valued they are and rewarding them out of the blue is light years better. Wouldn't you feel the same way if you were a client?

4. <u>Offer them something new</u>. People are always interested in something new. Think of it. When we run into a friend of ours, we say, *"what's new?"* We don't say, *"tell me the same thing you've been doing for the last couple of months"*.

    People are always interested in what's new and different. They don't want to hear about something they already know about. So, by offering clients a "new" type of massage you're offering, you're going to get their attention.

5. <u>Only contact your best clients</u>. This is a way to make clients feel special. Mention that this letter is only going to your most valued clients. This isn't going out to every Tom, Dick, and Harry. This is only going to your best clients as a way to thank them.

6. <u>Available to them before the general public</u>. This gives them a feeling of elitism. Everyone wants something before others can have it.

   When you offer something of value to your best clients before you make it available to others, they feel appreciated, important, recognized, and special. But when you make something available to everyone at the same time, it loses its impact.

7. <u>Set a time frame</u>. Give a time frame of about two weeks for them to take advantage of your offer. You *MUST* give them a sense of urgency. If not, they don't take it that seriously. By saying that this will be made available to everyone after a certain date, it inspires people to respond faster.

I understand that this probably seems confusing reading the format of a letter before seeing an actual example.

The next step shows you an example. <u>This will all make perfect sense *very* soon</u>.

I just needed you to get familiar with the concept of *The Guinea Pig Method* first in order to fully understand why it works so well.

Chapter 5

THE #1 EASIEST WAY TO HAVE A *TON* OF MASSAGE CLIENTS HANDED TO YOU JUST FOR ASKING

After you've found work space that you'd enjoy having a massage practice in, what's next? Let's assume that you've found a hair salon that you can use for your practice.

The room is nice, the owner is open to your marketing ideas (*which you'll learn shortly*), and it looks like a good arrangement for everyone. What do you do next?

First, let me tell you what *not* to do. Don't simply put out business cards and brochures on the counter the way every other therapist does. You're just wasting your time and money. You won't get clients that way. You need to be proactive and take matters into your own hands by first introducing yourself to the staff.

What you want to do now is to give a letter of introduction to everyone who works there – the stylists, the receptionists, the nail techs – everyone.

Briefly introduce yourself in the letter and offer each person a free half-hour sample of your massage session.

<u>This accomplishes two things</u>:

1. You'll get to personally meet every single employee at the salon. They'll now be much better acquainted with you and know first-hand what your massage sessions are like
2. These people will soon become your ambassadors and will be eager to promote you *(more on how that's done shortly)*

An example of this letter is found on the following page. It's also an example of *The Guinea Pig Method*:

Attach small bag
of Ice Breakers
mints

"Thought This Would Be A Fun Way To Break The Ice Between Us!"

Here's A Quick Letter To Introduce Myself And Ask If You'd Like To Be A 'Guinea Pig' For My New Massage Session In Exchange For Your Feedback

Dear (employee's first name),

Hi! My name is (your name) and I'm the new massage therapist here at (name of location). I thought attaching a bag of *Ice Breakers* mints would be a fun way to introduce myself and "break the ice" between us. I was also wondering if you'd be <u>interested in being a 'guinea pig' for a new massage</u> I've recently created.

If you're feeling stiffness in your neck, shoulders, lower back, arms, and wrists from work, I have a *really* cool new massage session that you're gonna *LOVE* that specializes on relieving these areas. Since <u>many hair stylists experience problems in these areas</u>, I thought that a fun way for us to meet would be to offer you a

COMPLIMENTARY 30-MINUTE SESSION FOR MY NEW *'RAPID RELIEF'* MASSAGE

This massage is *really* different. It focuses strictly on the areas that drive many people nuts like tension headaches, *'knotted up'* shoulders, stiff necks, and Carpal Tunnel Syndrome. And the best part is, it's designed to <u>relieve these symptoms</u> *in minutes!*

The only thing I'm asking for in exchange is your feedback and hearing exactly what kind of relief you experienced. I'm nervous because I haven't offered this session to the public yet and, honestly, I thought <u>you'd be a great 'guinea pig' for me to test these new techniques on first</u>!

Many salon professionals experience annoying stiff necks and shoulders, tightness in their wrists, and sore lower backs from their job. I thought this would be a great win/win for us – I get to practice my new session, and **you get a complimentary massage** and tell me your opinion of it. *Sound good?*

Also, if you have any questions about the session or about any muscle discomfort you may be feeling, I'd love to hear from you. Feel free to call me at (your number) or email me at (your email). I'd be happy to answer any questions you may have.

Thanks, (their name), and I hope to hear from you soon!

(your name), Massage Practitioner

There are six very important points that are included in this letter that must be followed:

1. Attach A Physical Object. This seemingly silly item actually plays a *huge* role in getting people's attention. Why?

   For one thing, a three dimensional item draws the reader's eyes to the letter like a magnet and instantly creates interest. This is extremely important!

   This arouses natural curiosity. You don't have to convince people to read the headline when they see an object attached to it. It's instinct.

   How many times have you ever gotten a letter in the mail with an object attached to it? If you ever did, didn't it automatically grab your attention? I'm sure you at least read the headline to see what this is all about.

   People have short attention spans and are constantly bombarded with messages and advertisements from every direction. You need to do everything you can to get and keep their attention.

   There is nothing that I've found that works better than a physical object attached to a letter, which will grab their attention and arouse curiosity.

2. Use Headlines And Sub-Headlines. Most massage therapists make the mistake of starting off a letter with their name and contact information at the top.

   This is *wrong, wrong, wrong!*

It is imperative that you immediately give the reader a solid reason to continue reading. The way to do this is by using headlines.

In this example, I tied the main headline with the object that I've attached – in this case, a small zip-lock bag of Ice Breakers mints. This will instantly grab their attention.

Next, I use a sub-headline that briefly states what this letter is all about – introducing myself and offering them a benefit which is a free half-hour massage session.

3. <u>Introduce Yourself</u>. For my opening paragraph, I quickly introduce myself in a lighthearted way by linking the object to my intro. This is a guaranteed way to get their attention. How could anyone not continue reading?

4. <u>Reason Why You're Contacting Them</u>. Notice how I'm not offering them a free massage for no reason. Believe it or not, many people don't take you up on a totally free massage.

   They usually think, *"what's the catch?"* In this case, there is a catch – I want their feedback on this 'new' massage session I've designed. It would also be a fun way to meet and get to know each other.

5. <u>Massage Session That Focuses On Problem Areas That Hair Stylists Have</u>. Also, I'm not just offering a free session for just Swedish massage. That's boring and doesn't spark interest. This session focuses on problems that many hair stylists suffer from. This really catches their eye.

6. <u>Include Your Contact Information</u>. At the end of the letter, I included my email address or suggested that if they have any questions about the massage, muscle aches, etc. This is also *very critical!*

   The reason is because if someone contacts you with a question, what they're really saying is, *"I really want to get a massage from you, but I just need a little more convincing."*

   The more they feel a connection with you, the more comfortable they'll feel getting a massage from you.

Now, how do you make sure that every employee gets this letter? First, ask the salon owner how many employees there are. Depending on the size of the business, there may only be a few.

Find out the first names of all of the employees, address a letter to each of them personally ("Dear _____"), and place it in an envelope with their name hand-written on the front.

The letters can either be left in a place where each employee is likely to find it or the salon owner/manager can hand them out.

Chapter 6

THE HIDDEN TRICK TO ATTAINING AS MANY LOYAL AMBASSADORS OF YOUR MASSAGE PRACTICE AS YOU WISH

The next few tasks actually aren't in a specific order because you're going to be doing a number of things simultaneously, but for the sake of clarity I'll put them in an order for now.

Let's start with giving away free half-hour sessions to your co-workers. These people are crucial to spreading the word about how wonderful your massage sessions are. They're going to be *your* ambassadors.

Word of mouth is the best form of marketing that you can do. What someone else says about you carries far more weight than what you say about you, as you'll soon learn throughout this course.

However, you simply cannot afford to sit back and assume that people are going to go out of their way to talk about you just because they liked your massage. You *must* be proactive and help stimulate this process as much as you can.

This Is Where Everything Starts Getting Kicked Into High Gear!

So let's now assume that you've worked on a few co-workers and they raved about how great that massage felt. Now what?

Let me first backtrack a little and quickly explain a few phrases – underline joint ventures and underline endorsement letters. *Endorsement letters? Joint ventures?*

Pretty boring terms, huh? So what exactly are they?

An endorsement letter is a letter of endorsement from a business owner or service provider *(such as a hair stylist, in this case)* to their existing customers which talks about you and your practice.

For example, a hair stylist can mail or hand out a letter to their clients that looks like it's written by them *(but is actually written by you)* offering their customers a free 15-20 minute massage with you as a thank you for being such loyal customers.

The letter goes on to say how wonderful your massage sessions are, how good you treated this person, how long you've known each other, etc.

This works for many reasons. Their customer already trusts that person. They already have a good relationship with each other. Those customers are much more likely to believe what that person says about your practice than what you say about your practice.

There is *instant* credibility and believability.

Why would a person personally endorse someone who wasn't reputable, reliable and gave great service? They wouldn't. It would only hurt *their* business and credibility.

<u>There are three powerful reasons why this benefits everybody</u>:

1. The service provider (*a hair stylist, in this case*) looks good to their customers by appearing as if they purchased the free 15-20 minute massage. It shows good will to their customers.

     a. In addition, the hair stylist doesn't write it. *You* will. They simply look the letter over and approve it. There is absolutely no extra work for them to do.

2. Their customers are getting a free gift with absolutely no strings attached as a thank you for being such good customers. This helps strengthen the bond between the business and their customers.

3. You benefit by acquiring new clients – which cost you *nothing* to acquire - that you can now nurture into lifetime clients.

     Also, you'll have new names and addresses to add to your mailing list to <u>continually market to</u> so that you always stay at the top of their minds when they think about massage.

<u>And here's what *joint ventures* are</u>...

A joint venture is when the other professional or business owner gets something in return whenever one of his/her customers buys something beyond the free 15-20 minute massage.

For example, your co-workers could get a percentage for every one of their hair or nail clients who book their first massage session with you *(not including the freebie)*. So now there's a financial incentive for your co-workers as well.

The more they promote you, the more commission they receive in addition to building a stronger relationship with their own customers.

Setting up endorsement letters and joint ventures *alone* are incredible ways to get other professionals and businesses to promote your practice. *See how easy these two methods work?*

So let's now go back to what exactly you do after you give a knock-out massage session to one of your new co-workers...

Within the next few days after they've received their complimentary massage, you now want to approach them with the idea of helping you promote your massage practice and explain how this will benefit them as well.

At this point you should feel comfortable enough to explain an endorsed letter arrangement. You probably won't have to do much convincing at all because they're already familiar and comfortable with you.

Most of them will have no problem at all helping you jumpstart your massage practice – as long as there's something in it for them, as you'll soon see.

They know what it's like getting a practice going and if you scratch their back, they'll scratch yours. You're about to learn the smoothest way to do this.

On the following page is an example of what your request for an endorsement letter should look like:

"Would You Like To Strengthen Your Relationship With Your Clients Without Doing Any Work?"

Hi (name)!

This is (your name). I just wanted to take a moment to thank you for taking advantage of your complimentary massage session the other day. I hope that you received some much deserved stress relief. I also have a fun promotional idea that can be extremely beneficial for both you and your customers by <u>giving your customers a special gift without costing you any time or effort and making you look *great* at the same time</u>.

I'd like to know if you would be kind enough to hand out to your clients a special "thank you" letter and gift certificate giving them a free 15-minute massage with me for being such loyal clients.

The letter also briefly explains the stress relief you experienced from my massage session and how you believe they would benefit from using my services, which is why you're giving them a free gift certificate for a free 15-minute massage session as a special gift from you.

The gift certificates and letter will be supplied by me. There's absolutely nothing your customers will never have to purchase anything. I thought it's a great opportunity for you to give something back to your clients and also a way to help me gain more exposure for my new massage practice. The truth is, it is much more advantageous to build a practice through referrals from professionals and new friends such as yourself.

Not only that, but for every one of your clients who book their first hour-long massage session with me after their complimentary session, you will receive $5 to thank you for taking the time to help promote my new massage practice here at (name of salon).

If this sounds like an interesting, win/win idea you'd like to pursue, I'd love to discuss it with you in more detail and answer any questions you may have. Please stop by to see me when I'm in, or feel free to call me at (your phone number) anytime.

Thanks, (name), and I look forward to hearing from you soon!

Let me briefly explain why this letter works so well.

Remember...

What's in it for them? Why should they take the time to do this?

This type of promotional arrangement strengthens their relationship with their customers by giving away a "free" gift as way of saying thank you with absolutely nothing they have to buy.

Their customers benefit by receiving a free 15-minute massage with no strings attached. <u>It's an unexpected free gift that appears as if the hair stylist paid for it</u>.

You're also explaining why you're doing this. Most of your business comes from referrals and is mutually beneficial rather than spending money on advertising that rarely pays off. There's no extra work they have to do. You're going to write the endorsement letter that is "coming from them".

There is also an incentive for them. Every single person who works at the salon should receive a copy of this letter – the hair stylists, receptionists, nail techs, etc. If the salon owner decides to mail them out, you can also offer to pay the postage. If they mailed an endorsement letter to 100 people, that's only $46.

<u>*Here's an extremely important point to remember...*</u>

It Is WAY More Effective To Spend $46 In Postage To Target 100 People Who Receive A Personalized Letter Endorsing You From A Local Business That Those People Already Frequent And Trust As Opposed To Placing An Ad In A Newspaper That Targets Thousands!

Just think of how much more effective that will be as opposed to spending a small fortune for an advertisement placed in the weekly community paper that only strangers see.

This is a concept that a lot of therapists have a hard time grasping. I talk to many therapists who say they'd rather spend a few hundred dollars *(that they usually don't have and have to put on a credit card)* for a newspaper advertisement than use direct mail.

Their reasoning is, *"Well, I can reach a lot more people with a newspaper advertisement and there's no way I could reach the same amount of people affordably with direct mail."*

On the surface, it sounds logical. But let's look at this through real life. Let's say that you wanted to place an ad in your local free weekly community paper. For the sake of numbers, let's say that the paper has a circulation of 50,000.

Let's also assume that you're going to place an ad that resembles something like this:

> *Serenity Day Spa. 123 Main St. Swedish, Reflexology, Hot Stone. Licensed & Insured. 20% Off First Visit With This Ad. (555) 555-5555. 'Healing The World One Massage At A Time'*

This is the typical massage advertisement that you see. The first problem is assuming that all 50,000 actually received the paper and brought it in their house. This doesn't always happen.

Some people aren't home for a few days. Some homes and apartments are empty. Some people are too lazy to even bring the paper inside and just leave it on their curb for days *(ever notice that?)* Sometimes the papers get ruined because of weather. So that eliminates a certain percentage.

And just because people bring the paper into their house, that doesn't guarantee that all of these people are reading it. Some people won't read the paper at all. They either forget about it or immediately throw it out. That eliminates even more people.

Some people only read the articles or the classified section and don't even *glance* at advertisements. Even *more* people who won't see your ad. Some people *do* scan everything in the paper. However, just because you placed an ad doesn't necessarily mean that it will catch people's eyes.

Most ads are black & white and blend in with every other ad in the paper. So even if someone might be interested in your ad, they may easily overlook it. And if your ad resembles every other ad like the one I described on the previous page, it has even *less* of a chance of standing out.

And let's not forget about the thousands of people who have absolutely *no* interest in getting a massage at all no matter how well the ad is written. When you combine all those factors, how many people are actually seeing your ad *and* are interested enough to make an appointment with you? Not very many.

That large number of 50,000 doesn't sound like a lot now, does it? <u>You end up paying hundreds of dollars to hopefully attract just a few people</u>. This is why it's so vitally important to have others promote you as much as you can through endorsement letters and referrals.

Chapter 7

THE *ONE* LETTER THAT WILL ATTRACT AS MANY CLIENTS AS YOU WANT, NON-STOP, EVERY DAY OF THE WEEK, FOR THE REST OF YOUR CAREER

I want to now show you exactly how powerful getting a personal endorsement is through the eyes of a potential client. The reason I'm doing this is because so many therapists don't take this method seriously even when they've learned how it works.

Most therapists continually try to attract new clients by placing ads in their newspaper, setting up a web site without first learning Search Engine Optimization, handing out flyers, leaving a stack of business cards somewhere, or hoping that others will talk about them.

Let me ask you a very important question:

"What's The <u>ONE</u> Thing That The Above Mentioned Marketing Methods Have In Common?"

The answer is that there is absolutely *NO* connection between the prospect and the massage therapist!

I don't want *YOU* to make this mistake.

Using the typical marketing methods that everybody uses, the therapist is hoping that their ad is good enough so that the person seeing it will call for an appointment.

<u>But what would get *your* attention more</u>:

a. An ad for a massage therapist you saw in the newspaper
b. A personalized letter endorsing a massage therapist that came from your hair stylist *(or chiropractor/personal trainer/yoga instructor/nail technician, etc)*?

The letter, obviously. How could it not?

On the following page is an example of this style of endorsed letter that hair stylists will be handing out to their clients, then I'll describe why this works so well:

"Here's A *FREE* Gift For Being Such A Fantastic Client!"

Dear Friend,

As one of my most valued clients, I wanted to give you a special gift as my way of saying thank you!

I just received a massage recently from *(your name)*, our new massage therapist, and not only did the muscle knots in my shoulders go away, but I haven't felt this relaxed in months! I soon learned just how wonderful of an addition *(your name)* is to our staff. He/she is professional in every way, extremely friendly, has a very comfortable environment, and most importantly, he/she relieved my shoulder stiffness (that I thought would never go away), quickly and without any discomfort.

I was so impressed with him/her, that I wanted to let my clients know that if they are experiencing any muscle aches and pains, or just want some badly needed stress relief, they should see (your name). So I've decided to give some of my most valued clients such as yourself a gift certificate for a **FREE** 15-minute neck and shoulder massage session with *(your name)*.

There is absolutely no obligation tied to this gift certificate. This is just something I thought you would really enjoy and a way for me to give you a much appreciated 'thank you' for your business.

Just stop by the front desk on your way out today or call us at (555)-555-5555 to schedule your **FREE** 15-minute neck and shoulder massage with *(your name)*. Please hurry, though. This complimentary session offer is only good until (red stamped date). I'd love for you to experience the same muscle relief that I did, and his/her time slots are filling up fast.

Thank you again for being such a great client. *Your business is much appreciated!*

Sincerely,

(name)

P.S. – Never received a massage before? Not sure what to expect? *(your name)* has a great booklet for you to read titled, *"What To Expect During Your First Massage Session"* to answer any questions you may have. You can pick up your **FREE** copy at our front desk.

This letter can easily be modified to fit whatever type of establishment you're going to be working at – a chiropractic office, day spa, hair salon, etc. Also, you can make the offer to be whatever you want. It can also be a certificate for half-off their first session.

Anyway, let's view this letter through the eyes of a client. If you received a personal letter of endorsement for a massage therapist that came from your favorite hair stylist, wouldn't *you* be more inclined to use the services of this person rather than calling an ad that you saw in the newspaper?

Wouldn't it naturally carry more credibility and believability? People are much more likely to use a recommendation from a service provider who you already know and trust.

You'll Have Instant Credibility In The Minds Of Prospects Before You Even Meet Them!!!

It doesn't get any better than that! And not only that, but if this person never received a massage before and is a little nervous about what to expect, there's a free booklet for them that answers any questions they may have. *Cool, huh?*

Another way that these letters and gift certificates can be distributed is by having the receptionists hand them out to all clients. Just make some minor adjustments to the letter.

How do you keep track of where new clients came from? Put a code number on the bottom corner of each gift certificate.

For example, if a stylist's name is Mary, you can code them M01, M02, M03, and so on. Code them whichever way works best for you. *Just remember to keep records.*

To wrap this chapter up, can you see how much more effective this method is? The prospect is getting:

1. Personal letter endorsing *YOU* from someone they know and trust
2. A free 15-minute massage with no strings attached
3. Recognized and thanked for being such a great client

3 Most Vital Pieces Of Information You Need To Acquire From 1st Time Clients Before You Even Touch Them

When new clients start calling to schedule their free introductory massage session, you *MUST* have them fill out a basic health questionnaire.

<u>There are three important reasons for this</u>:

1. To find out if they've ever had a massage session in the past.
2. To find out where they may be experiencing aches and pains.
   And the most important one...
3. To get their mailing address!

Let me start off by pointing out something that most massage therapists do which sabotages their practice – *not asking for a mailing address!*

It's critical that <u>you *must* ask for their mailing address at the top of the health questionnaire</u> that first-time clients fill out. I'm amazed at the number of businesses that don't ask for this.

How else are you supposed to promote yourself if you don't have your client's contact information? You can't. The vast majority of people *will* leave their name and address, so don't feel awkward about asking for it.

As you're looking over their health questionnaire, notice if they've ever received a massage in the past or not. Also notice where they're having any aches and pains. *(This actually has more to do with your marketing than in finding out about any contraindications. 99% of the people you ever work on will be fine with getting a massage)*

Keep These Two Answers In Mind Because They're Going To Play An Important Part In Influencing Them To Book A Longer Session With You

As you start working on your new client, make some small talk about any muscle aches and pains they may have *(which for 95% of them will most likely be somewhere in their neck and shoulder area)* and find out if they've received a massage before.

This information is crucial to gaining some key insights as to how to get them to book a full hour-long session with you after their complimentary session.

What You Say And Do After Their Introductory Session Is Over Is Vitally Important!!

Unfortunately, most therapists simply thank the client, hand him/her a business card and/or brochure and say, *"Have a nice day"* as they're leaving.

This is where so many potential long term clients are unfortunately lost forever. Most massage therapist sit back and hope that these clients will call again for another appointment.

The good news is that you won't be developing this bad habit. I'm going to show you 4 easy ways to get clients to rebook with you.

Why Your Client's Name Are The Sweetest Words They'll Ever Hear

I wasn't sure if this should be a chapter or not, but I didn't know where to put it. Anyway, it's an important point - always repeat your client's name a few times.

This is a powerful yet overlooked psychological tool that helps clients to feel bonded to you. When you actually repeat a person's name a few times during their session, they instantly feel connected to you.

As Dale Carnegie once said,

"Remember That A Person's Name Is To That Person The Sweetest And Most Important Sound In Any Language"

I couldn't agree more. So then, use it to your advantage – and it costs *nothing* to do.

You can say things during the session like, *"Nice to meet you, Mary... How does this pressure feel, Mary... It was really nice meeting you, Mary..."* and so on.

You don't want to repeat it too often, but saying it just a few times will subconsciously make them feel more connected with you.

I mean, don't you always feel just a little more connected to someone if they remember and repeat your name during a conversation? We all do. It's human nature.

Remember, what we want to do is start developing a relationship. Make them feel like a name and not a number.

Here's another cool trick you can use:

I like to talk to new clients as if I've known them for ten years. I picture that person as someone I already know well and am very comfortable with.

It works! So use this little psychological tool to your advantage during their introductory session.

The 3 Sentences That Subconsciously Influence Your Clients To Rebook With You *Immediately* Without Ever Having To Ask Them

Trying to persuade a client to book again always feels awkward, in my opinion. Even experienced therapists admit to me that they don't do a good enough job in asking clients to rebook.

I was never good at it either until I finally came up with a short paragraph that works like a charm.

The idea behind it is to subtly and subconsciously get your new client to come to a decision in their own mind that they *really, really* should rebook with you before they leave.

You see, when a person feels that he/she has the freedom to make up their own mind about something, they now have a *conviction* that their decision is the right one. However, if *you* try to convince someone why they should take a certain action, it doesn't have the same impact.

Whenever you work on someone for the first time, say something at the end of the session that relates a specific problem they've just complained about, like neck and shoulder pain.

So at the end of a session, you should always say something like this:

"You know, Mary, now that I have an idea of what's going on with your muscles, I've recently learned this fantastic new massage technique that relieves real stubborn neck and shoulder pain in less than one session. When you schedule your next session, we can try this technique and focus solely on your neck and shoulders, if you wish, and help you work out this problem. It's given some great relief to a few of my clients and I really think your upper back will get some much needed relief from it as well."

Let me break this paragraph down and reveal why it's so important...

First, you're letting them know that you've just learned this incredible new massage technique that deals with the area of the body that they are having a problem with *(what a coincidence!)*

This gives you segue into bringing up the topic of booking another session with you. It's not enough just to say, *"You know, another session would probably be good for you."*

This is what the majority of massage therapists say to a new client. In this case, we have a solid reason to suggest that they experience this new bodywork technique because it solves one of *their problems*.

We're not trying to *sell* them a product or service that they have no interest in. We know for certain that they're currently experiencing neck and back pain because they told you so.

Next, notice that I said, *"When you schedule your next session..."* instead of, *"If you schedule another session..."*

This plants a little seed in their mind that subtly implies that they *are* going to book another session with you. It's a subconscious way to steer them in the right direction.

But if you say, *"If you'd like to book another session..."* it gives them an opportunity to say no. They have to make either a yes or no decision.

Instead, we want them to believe that they're *going* to rebook, not *if* they rebook. This makes the process easier for you, too, because you don't feel awkward about *selling* or getting them to upgrade. Also, inside of the first sentence, I've included a powerful headline. Let me quickly point this out:

"...fantastic new massage technique that relieves real stubborn neck and shoulder pain in less than one session."

You can take this part of the sentence and run it as a headline in a classified ad with a way to contact you and, believe me, you'll get inquiries. It would look like this:

> **Fantastic New Massage Technique Relieves Stubborn Neck & Shoulder Pain In Less Than One Session!** For FREE eBook, go to.

So I very cleverly inserted a benefit driven headline *(or bullet point)* into the body copy. *Nifty, huh?*

I then wrap it up by telling them how a few of my regular clients received some much needed relief with this technique and I think that they would enjoy it, too. Nothing heavy. No feeling 'pushy'.

This, of course, can be tweaked to fit your personality. Isn't that a simple way to easily move the person into the next step? See how this is painless and not awkward at all?

You'd be amazed at how many people say, *"Yeah, that's a good idea. Let's do that."* It also gives them something to look forward to the next time. You're giving them a solid reason as to *why* they should schedule with you again as opposed to just saying to them, *"Thank you and come again"* as they walk out the door.

You're gently leading toward making another session and letting them know what they'll expect the next time they see you.

The next chapter shows you how to take all of the guesswork out of your marketing. You're going to seem like you're reading your clients' minds like a psychic.

Chapter 8

TWO SECRETS THAT TAKE *ALL* OF THE GUESSWORK OUT OF YOUR MARKETING AND TELL YOU *EXACTLY* WHAT EACH OF YOUR CLIENTS WANT AT ZERO COST

Now we're going to start getting into some really powerful techniques that will instantly get others magnetically hooked into your marketing material.

If you've ever sat down and tried to write a marketing message but your mind just went blank and you didn't know what to write, these two secrets are going to solve that problem forever.

These are the most sure-fire ways to know in detail exactly what each individual client wants, likes and dislikes. These secrets take almost 100% of the guesswork out of all of your marketing, and it doesn't cost even a dime!

The first secret is...

Keep Accurate Notes For Each Client And Prospect

Many therapists fall into the trap of not keeping constantly updated notes about their current and past clients. Have a separate sheet of paper and write down anything you can about this person and the session.

- *What type of massage did you do?*
- *What type of pressure was it? Deep tissue? Effleurage?*
- *What did you talk about?*
- *What comments did they make?*
- *Did they seem interested in making another appointment?*
- *What problem areas in their muscles did they point out to you?*
- *How did they describe their pain/discomfort?*
- *What are the exact words they use?*
- *Did they talk about their home life?*
- *What are their hobbies?*

If you're not exactly sure about certain information, just jot down as much as you can about whatever comes to mind. This takes only a minute to do and will give you all the information you need when you're marketing your practice.

For example, here's a basic list of things I write down:

- ✓ How they found me (*through a referral, sales letter, redeeming a gift certificate, etc.*)
- ✓ Date of first session
- ✓ Date of each additional session
- ✓ Discounts (*if any*)
- ✓ Length of session
- ✓ Parts of the body I worked on (*neck and back only, full*

body, etc.)
- ✓ Where did I see this client *(in my office or in their home)*
- ✓ What we talked about *(VERY important!)*
- ✓ How they described their pain/discomfort

So if a client made a comment, like, *"Boy, I'll bet an entire hour on my feet would feel great!"* - I've got her! I'll write that info down in that person's notes. Then, if she wasn't able to make another appointment with me before she left her current appointment, I now know *precisely* which type of massage she would like to receive in the future.

For example, if this person was a regular client of mine and always booked an appointment with me once a month and then hasn't made an appointment in a few months, I can now mail her a sales letter for a reflexology package. I already know for a fact that she'll be *extremely* interested in that type of bodywork.

I can now contact her and let her know about a new massage package that she might be interested in *(which, in this example, would be my reflexology package)*. When done this way, response rates skyrocket!

An example of notes could look like this – the first sentence is a little background on the client, and the next is what you could write about this person's latest session:

(Jane Smith, 60 yr old, mobile client, date of first session – 02/20/95, usually see every 1-2 months, likes full body work)

(today's date)...wanted more attention on lower back today from overwork. Loved the fascia rolling and neck traction.

Also mentioned that she likes it when I start session on her feet...

Now, if you haven't worked on Jane in a few months and you wanted to contact her, you could send her a letter offering a new massage package that you think she would really like which focuses on her lower back.

You then describe a little bit about what she'll experience during this massage. In this case, you start describing how the session starts off with you working on her feet. That alone will grab this particular person's attention. You know from your notes that this client likes her feet worked on *first*.

Here's another example...

Let's say that you're working on someone for the first time and ask them if they've ever received a hot stone massage, and they say something like, *"Yeah. One time on my honeymoon 5 years ago. It was great."*

Jot that information down! You can tie that into a future sales letter. And what a coincidence – *you just happen to know hot stone massage!*

Now you can easily market a hot stone massage special to this person. <u>And here's the secret to hooking them</u> - you now send this person a sales letter that says...

"...I remember the last time I saw you back in July, you told me how the only time you received a hot stone massage was on your honeymoon. Well, <u>I have some great news for you</u>! I have a brand new hot stone massage package that I'd love to tell you about..."

Do you believe that your response rate will increase if you marketed to your clients in this way? There's no doubt it will. This is as focused on a client as you can get.

They'll Be Unbelievably Impressed That You Remembered That Information!

This speaks volumes about how attentive you are to their individual likes and wants.

So those are the reasons why jotting down a few brief notes on every client can make all of your marketing much more effective without doing hardly any extra work and with <u>zero cost</u>.

Now, the next secret shows you exactly what words to use in your marketing material. So if you're thinking...

"That makes sense, Jeff, but I still have a difficult time putting it into words. I can't even write a grocery list"

This is where most therapists get stuck. They know they have an incredible massage to offer, but they don't know how to effectively describe their massage in a way that will get people to respond.

Now, there *are* copywriting books and courses available. I highly recommend investing in a few of those – but I also know that, in all honesty, that's probably not going to happen (*hey – I'm just keeping it real*).

But there is a much easier, faster, more fun, and *FREE* way to learn how to do this.

And the neat part is that I've never seen this taught in any copywriting courses or books (*and I've invested in a lot of them*).

But first, let me as you if you've ever experienced this...

Have you ever been to a psychic, tarot card or palm reader – whether that person was legitimate or a real good fake – and that person said something that stopped you dead in your tracks and you thought to yourself, *"How the hell did he/she know that?"*

If you've ever experienced this, time seemed to stand still for a moment, didn't it? It's happened to me a few times and it freaked me out. *"Is this person for real? Or is he/she a very good fake?"*

Maybe it didn't come from a psychic. It could've come from a religious speaker, salesperson, mentalist – anybody. You're *instantly* tuned into what this person has to say next, aren't you? Nobody has to convince you to pay attention to this person. *They got your attention!*

Why did you experience this? It's because that person communicated something to you in a way that spoke to your core. It resonated something inside of you.

So let me ask you this...

How would you like to never have to "convince" anyone to get a massage from you ever again? That would be perfect, wouldn't it? You just say whatever it is that you say and they make an appointment.

This is what every massage therapist strives for. Unfortunately, it doesn't happen that way... *until now!*

If you love doing massage but HATE writing marketing material because you don't know what to say and just freeze up, <u>this is what you do to attract clients and prospects like crazy regardless of your competition</u>:

Google keywords such as *pain management forums, pain relief message boards, chronic pain forums* – phrases like that. Those aren't the only keywords, but you get the idea.

Start paying attention to the *exact* words and phrases that people use to describe their pain. Look at the posts as well as the comments. Why is this so important? Because these words come straight from the horse's mouth.

When you use the exact language that others use to describe their situation, they're going to instantly feel a connection with you.

<u>Here's another way to put it...</u>

"If You Can Describe A Person's Situation Better
Than They Can, Now You Got 'Em!"

So when you're reading different forums, write down any commonalities that you find. You're going to be surprised at how different they are from how the massage organizations, schools, magazines, and brochures describe them.

Let me describe a scenario for you so that you totally understand what I mean. Let's say you're having lunch with a real close friend. During lunch, your friend starts complaining about headaches she always gets.

<u>Do you think she would describe her symptoms this way</u>:

"I believe my C1 and C2 vertebrae aren't in proper alignment. Also, the muscle fibers in my cervical area are causing trigger points that are referring to my temporal region."

Hell no!

<u>She would probably describe her headaches this way...</u>

"Mary, this goddamn headache has been killing me for two days! It feels like someone is stabbing my eyeball. I can't get any work done and my boss is going be pissed. It got so bad I snapped at the poor waiter at the restaurant last night. I don't know what else to do to make it go away."

<u>Now would you – as a massage therapist – say to her</u>:

"Well, Karen, the reason why you're experiencing severe headaches is probably because of trigger points firing from your cervical area into your temporal region that's causing a high amount of neurological activity. Myofascial Release removes unwanted toxins that impedes healing and brings harmony to your mind, body, and spirit, and gives you a better overall sense of well being."

Of course you wouldn't! I think your friend Karen would stab *YOU* in the eye if you worded it that way.

She would probably respond, *"...what?! Mary, I didn't under-stand a word of what you just said. I think my headache actually got worse from hearing that confusing gibberish. Thanks."*

However, notice that ALL marketing material for thera-pists to give to people are worded the same way. Every one of them. Without exception. Now if you wouldn't talk to a friend using confusing, boring gibberish that they can't relate to, then...

Don't Use It For Clients And Prospects!!

I don't give a rat's ass how many other therapists, day spas, and other body workers have this in their material. Let them bore the crap out of people. *YOU* won't!

So let's go back to the above example. Your friend Karen is talking about her headaches and you – a massage therapist – know how you can help her.

You'd probably respond to her like this:

"You're right, Karen. They're a bitch! Even doctors aren't sure how to treat them. And the only thing they do is pump you full of drugs that make you feel like a zombie, right? I might be able to help you out, though.

This guy Bob - A co-worker of my husband - also gets crip-pling migraines. I mean, he has to lay down in bed in complete darkness and total silence until it eases up, which is hard to do when you have two young kids at home. And he feels horrible because he finds himself taking it out on his family. Even after it subsides, he's absolutely drained of energy.

Anyway, a few months ago I learned this really cool massage technique that specializes in relieving those pain-in-the-ass migraine headaches. So I practiced this new technique on him and he told me a few weeks later that he hasn't had one since!

His mood improved, he's more productive at work, he doesn't have to take as much medication - even his wife and kids noticed a difference. If you're interested, I'd love to try this technique on you and see if you get similar results.

It's painless, takes only about 30-minutes, and you won't have to get it done 2-3 times a week forever like when you go to a chiropractor."

Doesn't that sound like a normal conversation? Can you see how a person suffering from severe headaches can relate to this kind of language?

If you were Karen, would gibberish like *myofascial release... trigger points... temporal region... a better overall sense of well being... toxins... neurological activity... mind, body, and spirit...* get your attention?

No they wouldn't. Only other massage therapists talk that way *(which even bore the shit out of me, too).*

Wouldn't the second example get you interested? It sounds more like a regular conversation, doesn't it? It empathizes by mentioning symptoms that others experience, it tells a story, gives results, and there's a simple offer to try it out without sounding like a salesperson.

This is what you'll find when you check out some of the pain management forums. Just remember to read the posts and comments from *real people* – not from doctors who use confusing and boring terminology.

Don't you relate better to health care professionals who can empathize with you and explain things in easy to understand, everyday language? We all do. And you can learn all this by observing chronic pain forums. There are plenty of them out there.

You'll see a dramatic difference in response rates when you relate to others and not go over their heads.

Let's go into more detail to give you a better understanding of why this is so important. First, let's start with the 'thank you letter'.

A thank you letter with a *real* signature *(not a printed one)* is one of the most overlooked yet extremely appreciated personal touches you can give a new client. It's easy, free and takes practically no time at all to do.

On the following page is an example of a 'thank you letter' that every first-time client of yours should receive:

"Welcome! Thank You! And Congratulations!"

WELCOME! As a new client of mine, I want to welcome you as a new friend of (you/your practice). I also want to *THANK YOU* for entrusting me with a role in helping you have a happier, healthier, and more stress-free life.

I also want to *CONGRATULATE* you for joining a growing community of people who are being proactive in their health and wellness. The benefits of receiving regular therapeutic massages are nothing short of amazing.

After you maintain a regular schedule of massage therapy, you'll notice dramatic differences in many aspects of your life such as having more restful sleep, increased energy throughout your day, and decreased muscle tension.

And as a special treat, I've also added a gift certificate made out in your name for a **FREE 15-minute massage session** that you can give to a family member, friend, or co-worker so that they can experience the same wonderful benefits as you have. This special gift certificate is good for a free 15-minute massage session or it can be applied as a discount toward an hour-long session, their choice.

I also want you to know that I'm available to answer any questions you may have about stress and/or muscle tightness. Feel free to email me anytime at (your email address). You'll receive a response from me within 24 hours.

It was a pleasure meeting you, and I'm looking forward to giving you more therapeutic massage sessions in the near future!

In good health,

(your name printed)

(signature in blue ink)

Let's examine this letter a little more closely. First, it welcomes the client as a new friend of your practice.

Second, it thanks the client for taking the time to see you and take advantage of their free massage session. This is important because most businesses don't take the time to thank and appreciate a new client/customer for their patronage.

Third, it tells them about the free gift certificate that's made out in their name that they can give to any friend or family member. This also makes the new client look good. If they *do* give this gift certificate to someone, it looks as if they paid for it.

Wouldn't *you* appreciate a totally free 15-minute massage session from a friend or family member?

Fifth, it lets them know that you're accessible. If they have any questions about massage or any aches and pains that they have, they can email you. This is more important than you may think because if someone emails you with a question, what they're really saying is...

"I really want to get a longer massage session from you, but I just need you to convince me a little more"

Chapter 9

HOW TO GET LOCAL BUSINESSES HAPPILY PROMOTING YOUR PRACTICE FOR <u>FREE</u>

The first thing I want you to do is to look over your entire database of clients - past and present. Write down the names of any that own or manage a local service-oriented business *(employees can be included, too)*. Try to think of at least 10.

If you can list more than 10, that's even better! You might be surprised at how many you already have.

<u>Examples Of Service-Oriented Businesses Are:</u>

1. Hair salons
2. Nail salons
3. Accountants
4. Travel agents
5. Real estate agents
6. Florists
7. Wedding planners/bridal shops
8. Chiropractors and other doctors

9. Martial arts instructors
10. Personal trainers
11. Yoga instructors
12. Health food store owners
13. Nutritionists
14. Bookstore owners
15. Restaurants
16. Pet groomers
17. Avon salespeople
18. Psychics

Practically any service-based business can work.

But there's a problem...

> *** What do you do if you don't have enough – or any – clients that are in a local service business? Hang tight. We're going to tackle that minor bump in the road soon.***

Next, contact 3 of these clients and ask for a short testimonial. This is important because we're going to be using them in our future marketing.

Don't be nervous about this! People are more than happy to give a testimonial if you simply ask them.

If any of them happen to be scheduled with you this week for a massage, you can wait until then - *but only for the rest of this week*. Don't wait any longer than that.

You can call, email, send a letter, or ask them in person.

If you don't know what to say, just say something like:

"Hi Mary! It's (your name). How are you? I'd like to ask you for a favor, if you don't mind. I'd like to know if you'd be so kind to write a brief testimonial about the stress relief you've experienced since becoming a client of mine.

I'm putting together a testimonial booklet spotlighting clients of mine who have a local service business, and I'd love to include a brief quote from you to use in a future promotion.

It's because of friends like you that keep my massage therapy center going strong, and I'd love to hear your positive experiences that I can show to others. Thank you so much, Mary. I really appreciate it.

Oh - I'm planning on printing up my testimonial booklet on (date) so if you can shoot me a quick email at (your email address) by (date), that would be great! Again, nothing too long - just a few before/after sentences. Thanks again!"

Of course, you can tweak it. It doesn't have to be verbatim. Make it fit your own voice.

This will work for 3 reasons:

- ✓ You *WILL* get testimonials just for asking.
- ✓ When they see that they'll be spotlighted in a booklet, it gives them even more incentive to give you one.
- ✓ They'll feel very appreciated. It's rare that a business takes the time to recognize and thank their clients.

One more thing - don't let them get back to you whenever they feel like it. It'll slip their minds. Make a date that's within a few days. If any of them don't know what to say, you can even write it for them as long as they approve it.

This step is critical because it's going to add to your validity when prospects start hearing about you. You're going to instantly appear as *the* massage authority in your area!

Remember - they HAVE to be from clients who own, manage, or are employed in a local service industry.

<u>If you're still feeling stuck finding people, here's another tip to help you</u>...

If you can't think of many current or past clients that you can write down, think of all of the service businesses in your area that you currently frequent. Think of family & friends that might be in a service business that you may have worked on while you were still in massage school.

For example, how about *your* family doctor? Or *your* dentist? Who cuts *your* hair? Do you have a brother-in-law who owns a service business?

This is the next best group that is almost guaranteed to help promote you – *and* you won't feel awkward approaching them!

The really cool part is that if you just get a few of them to promote you to their clients and customers... *you may not have to worry about promoting yourself ever again!*

<u>So before we get started, write down</u>...

10 Clients, Family, Friends, Or Neighbors That Are In A Local Service Related Industry:

1._____

2._____

3._____

4._____

5._____

6._____

7._____

8._____

9._____

10._____

Write Down 3 Of These Clients Or Friends That You Can Get A Testimonial From Immediately:

1._____

2._____

3._____

So, how do you contact these 10 *(or more)* people and what exactly do you say? *Easy!*

On the next page is a template that you can use as a letter or a script:

"Would You Like To Strengthen Your Relationship With Your Customers Without Doing Any Work Or Spending A Penny?"

Hi *(name)*!

This is (your name) from (name of your practice). How are you? I'm writing you because I have a unique promotional idea that can be extremely beneficial for your business by **giving your customers a special gift without costing you any money, time or effort, and making you look *great* at the same time**.

Here's what I have in mind:

I'd like to know if you would be kind enough to give your customers a special "thank you" letter and gift certificate for a free 15-minute massage session with me as a way of thanking them for being such loyal customers of yours.

The letter will be a "thank you" letter to your best customers *(or your entire database)* that briefly explains how you believe they will benefit from (you/your practice). They'll also receive a gift certificate for a free 15-minute massage session as a special gift from you.

The letter will be written by *me* and approved by *you* so there's absolutely no work for you to do *whatsoever*! (*A sample letter can be given to you*)

There's absolutely no catch and your customers will never have to purchase anything. I thought it would be a fun, easy, and **FREE** way for you to *really* look great by giving your customers a complimentary 15-minute massage session, and also a way to help me gain more exposure for my massage practice.

The truth is, it is much more meaningful to expand my practice through endorsements from great clients like you!

If this sounds like an interesting idea that you'd like to pursue, I'd love to discuss it with you in more detail and answer any questions you may have. I can be reached at (555)-555-5555 anytime.

Thanks, *(name)*, and I look forward to hearing from you!

(your name)

Let me briefly explain why this letter works so well. The most important thing to remember is...

What's in it for them? Why should they take the time to do this?

This type of arrangement strengthens their relationship with *their* customers by giving away a free gift as way of saying thank you with absolutely nothing they have to buy.

Their customers benefit by receiving a free 10-15 minute massage with no strings attached. <u>It's an unexpected free gift that appears as if the business owner paid for it.</u>

Remember – you can make the offer to be whatever you want. It can also be a certificate for half-off their first session.

You're also explaining why you're doing this. Most of your business comes from referrals and this type of arrangement is mutually beneficial rather than spending money on advertising that rarely pays off.

There's no extra work they have to do. You're going to write the endorsement letter that looks as if it's written by them.

You can even offer to pay the postage if they wanted to mail these letters instead. If they mailed to 100 customers, that's only $44.

It Is WAY More Effective To Spend $46 In Postage To Target 100 People Who Receive A Personalized Letter Endorsing <u>YOU</u> From A Local Business That Those People Already Frequent And Trust As Opposed To Placing An Ad In A Newspaper That Costs Hundreds Of Dollars!

Just think of how much more effective that will be as opposed to spending a small fortune on the typical advertisement placed in the weekly community paper!

Let me give you a few examples how this plays out in real life. Let's say that you have current clients who are in a service business who agreed to endorse you to their clients/customers.

One is a florist, one is a travel agent, and the other is a manicurist. They each agree to hand out thank you letters and gift certificates to just 20 of their best clients.

That's 60 gift certificates that could potentially be redeemed, right? Of course, not all of them will. But let's assume that 10 do *(and this is a conservative number)*.

Then let's assume that 5 of them book an hour-long session after their short freebie *(and they will when you implement the follow-up system that's taught later in this course)*.

If you charge $60 per hour, that's $300 you just made! And I'm not even talking about repeat bookings, referrals, gift certificate and other product sales, testimonials, etc.

And you now have 10 people that you can now nurture into lifelong clients *(those other 5 that didn't immediately book a longer appointment are NOT going to be lost, as you're going to soon learn)*.

And did it cost you any money? Nope. Any upfront advertising expenses? Nope. Did you have to go through the stress and cost of putting up a web site? Nope.

Now I want to talk about a problem that most massage therapists have and can't figure out why they're having it - getting family and friends to promote you...

Chapter 10

HOW TO EASILY GET YOUR FAMILY AND FRIENDS TO PROMOTE YOUR MASSAGE PRACTICE AND THE #1 REASON WHY THEY WON'T

One of the first things that massage therapists do when they're trying to promote themselves is to tell their family and friends about their new practice.

Many other marketers will give you the same advice. Although this may be true in theory, most businesses mess this up without realizing it.

The most common mistake that massage therapists make is handing out business cards to their family and friends and saying...

"If you know anyone who needs a massage, here's my card"

You may even offer them a freebie to help get the ball rolling.

The strange part is that many therapists have a hard time even giving away their massages for free! *Why is this so?*

The main reason why many therapists have a difficult time getting their friends and family to get a massage from them – even a free one – is because they feel uncomfortable getting one from person who is so close to them.

For example, it's awkward thinking about your brother-in-law rubbing your body with oil, isn't it? To them, getting a massage from you may just feel, well... *weird!* This is especially true if the therapist is male.

Also, they don't want to feel obligated to continue receiving massages from you or to hand out your business cards to others.

What if they didn't really like your massage? They're not going to tell you that they didn't care for it, but they're also not going to get another massage from you, either.

What if they did get a massage from you a few times and then stopped? They're going to know that you're wondering why they've stopped making appointments with you.

This is awkward for everyone, and that's why many people won't do business with family or close friends. It can be a sticky situation, especially when we're talking about rubbing people's bodies with oil.

But There Is A Way To Utilize Friends And Family In A Way That Is Comfortable And Beneficial For Both Of You

Here's how you do this...

Ask if you can give them a massage session in exchange for their comments and a short testimonial of how they felt after the session.

This is a much easier approach because there is a good reason behind it. You're looking for feedback and suggestions that you can use to improve your skills and asking if they would also please write a few sentences about their experience.

Explain that you're collecting testimonials to help promote your new massage practice and that this would be a cool way to 'bribe' your family and friends into getting a session.

The best group of family and friends to offer this to are ones who own a business. You can also tell them that the name of their business is going to be included in your marketing material (*more on this in a moment*).

Don't worry if none of your friends or family owns a local business. Just try to get as many friends and family to get a massage from you in exchange for their comments and testimonials.

What you now do with these testimonials is *very* important. Once you collect testimonials from your friends and family, make a booklet out of them.

This is probably the only time that I recommend using a brochure format. Give it a strong title like,

> *"12 Reasons Why These People Chose (your name) As Their Massage Therapist"*

*"Why These 12 People Chose (your name) To
Give Them Neck & Back Pain Relief"*

Inside will be 12 testimonials about your massage sessions and how great they felt afterward.

Once you have enough testimonials for a booklet, you now include this in your new client kit. Can you see why this works much better than the standard massage brochure?

And the great thing about this is that you'll continually be adding to it over time. Imagine how impressive it would be to a new client when they see a booklet of 47 testimonials raving about your massage practice.

This gets even better...

When you start getting more testimonials from clients who own local businesses, you can create a booklet with the title, *"Why These 18 Local Celebrities Choose (your name) As Their Massage Therapist"*.

The key word in the headline is *'Celebrities'*.

People are automatically attracted to celebrities and what they do. When someone opens this booklet, they see a list of 18 testimonies from local business owners.

This is even more impressive. Why would the owners of local businesses not only see you as their massage therapist but then give you glowing testimonials if they were unhappy with your services? They wouldn't. That's why this works so well.

Let's go back to focusing on your family and friends. Make a list of every friend or family member you're willing to give a free massage session to.

Contact these people however you wish – phone call, email, text, fax, person to person, letter – and say something like,

> *"Hi (name), it's (your name). I'd like to know if you'd be able to do me a favor. I (just graduated massage school / am revamping my current massage practice) and I need to practice a few techniques.*
>
> *I'm also trying to put together a booklet of testimonials of my massage sessions to give to people. Would you mind getting a free massage from me in exchange for any suggestions and comments about my massage techniques and then writing a few quick sentences about your experience? This will really help me get my practice off the ground and, hey, you get a free massage!"*

Can you see why that works so much better than simply handing people our business cards? When mentioned this way, both sides feel more comfortable about the exchange.

Even if only 5 friends and family members took you up on it, you now have 5 testimonials about you and your practice right off the bat. And if you really do accidentally screw something up, they're not going to care.

You can also do this whenever you learn a new massage technique. When you're ready to promote it, you can send out a sales letter to your database with the headline...

"How These 5 People Eliminated Their Lower Back Pain With My New (name of massage) Technique And How You Can Experience The Same Amazing Results"

...and include these 5 testimonials. The new massage technique you just learned will instantly be more credible and grab the reader's attention when you're promoting it. Clever little trick, isn't it? <u>And *none* of it is hype</u>!

THAT'S how you utilize your family and friends when starting a new practice or trying to promote a new massage technique you recently learned.

Chapter 11

WRAPPING IT ALL UP

Congratulations! You have already accomplished more than many of the practitioners who purchased this book have done.

What do I mean by that?

Unfortunately, many people who invest in a self-help book, home study course or seminar of any kind rarely get past their initial stage of excitement.

The rush usually wears off pretty quick.

Daily life takes over. Work and family life take precedence. Other priorities demand our attention. The day-to-day routines pick up right where they left off.

"I'll start reading that book tomorrow", most people say.

But tomorrow never comes.

The next thing they know, a book that could be potentially life-changing ends up sitting on a shelf collecting dust.

"*Tomorrow. Right after work. I promise*", they fool themselves into thinking. And what happens after work?

Throw something in the microwave for dinner. Spend some time with the spouse and kids. Watch some mindless TV before bed.
Now exhaustion sets in.

"*Oh, I forgot to start reading that book. All right. Tomorrow. I swear.*"

Within just a few days the book is completely forgotten about.

Not you!

But hold on. Acquiring specialized knowledge is only the first step toward your new or revitalized career. Taking action on what you've learned is the next.

You see, if you don't take consistent daily action on what you've learned, even if in small steps, you might as well not have invested the time and energy into a self-help book/CD/seminar/ home study course in the first place.

You can have this entire course memorized like the back of your hand, but it will mean *NOTHING* if you don't start taking action immediately.

Neither you, your clients nor the hundreds of future clients who would love your bodywork will benefit from the wealth of knowledge this course has given you if it isn't applied.

Please don't make the mistake that many other people make.

There are some people who *do* take the time to finish studying a course like this, but get frustrated and give up if they don't hit a home run right from the start.

The old saying, *"If it looks too good to be true, it usually is"* is correct. The reality is that it's *supposed* to take some time, effort, tweaking and testing to fit your business.

The good news is that you now have my *proven system* to make your practice as big and as successful as you want it to be.

The roadmap is already in your hands. All you have to do is follow it and don't give up!

If you invest just one hour a day consistently studying this course and applying the information it contains, you'll eventually reach your destination.

And this book will absolutely, without question guide you to a thriving career in massage – whether you desire a part-time or full-time practice.

I sincerely thank you from the bottom of my heart for investing in this book.

Feel free to email me any time with your questions and comments at jeff@instantmassagetherapypractice.com. I love corresponding with fellow massage therapists.

Hearing success stories from the many massage practitioners who have applied this information and have had their lives and careers turned around make it all worthwhile.

Take care and I hope to hear from you soon!

JEFF SAUERS BIO

Jeff Sauers has been a well respected massage therapist and relaxation expert for 16 years. He has worked with M.D.'s, Chiropractors and upscale spas as well as growing his own private practice.

After graduating from Massage Arts & Sciences Center of Philadelphia in 1993, Jeff continued his education by training in Neuromuscular, Myofascial Release, Craniosacral, Soft Tissue Pain Release and Reiki therapies.

He is also a contributing author for the massage marketing book, *"The Magic Touch"*. He was also a former contributor to MBU.com, writing monthly articles teaching massage therapists how to easily attract clients.

In 2007 Jeff was a guest speaker for GetMassageClients.com and had his marketing techniques featured in Massage Marketing Gold Newsletter.

In 2008 released the *Ultimate Massage Success Home Study Course*, a comprehensive marketing course for massage therapists.

In 2010 Jeff released two more marketing courses: *The Effortless Influence Course* and the *Hybrid Massage Therapy Practice Course*.

From 2008-2011 Jeff released a subscription-based monthly marketing newsletter and audio CD. In 2010 he was also a guest speaker for SuccessfulMassageTherapist.com and MassageNerd.com.